D1033066

THE GREAT DECISION

THE

The Secret History

GREAT DECISION

of the Atomic Bomb

MICHAEL AMRINE

G. P. PUTNAM'S SONS New York

Published simultaneously in the Dominion of Canada by Longmans, Green & Company, Toronto.

The Library of Congress has catalogued this book as follows:

Amrine, Michael. Great decision of the atomic bomb. New York, Putnam, 1959. 244 p. 23 cm. 1. World War, 1939–1945—Japan. 2. Atomic bomb. I. Title. D767.2.A5 940.5442 58–14036 ‡

MANUFACTURED IN THE UNITED STATES OF AMERICA

VAN REES PRESS • NEW YORK

for Renee

Acknowledgments

THE AUTHOR is indebted to Houghton-Mifflin Co. for permission to quote from *Triumph & Tragedy,* by Winston S. Churchill; to Whittlesey House, Copyright © 1950 by the Curtis Publishing Company, Copyright © 1950 by William D. Leahy, to quote from *I Was There* by Admiral William D. Leahy; to James F. Byrnes for permission to quote from *Speaking Frankly,* published by Harper & Bros.; to Thomas Y. Crowell to quote from *We Dropped the A-bomb,* by Merle Miller and Ave Spitzer; to McGeorge Bundy to quote from *On Active Service,* by Henry L. Stimson & McGeorge Bundy, published by Harper & Bros.; to William Hillman for permission to quote from *Mr. President,* by Harry S. Truman, published by Farrar, Straus and Young; to Time, Inc. for permission to quote from *Years of Decision* by Harry S. Truman; to Oxford University Press, Inc. for permission to quote from *Atomic Quest,* by Arthur Compton.

Contents

THE GREAT DECISION

1.

"Quickly and Quietly"

AT FIVE O'CLOCK this spring afternoon the Vice-President was running—alone—through the basement of the Capitol Building.

Harry S. Truman was sixty years old, but he did not think of his heart or his health as he trotted through the long, cool corridor. Mr. Truman, as if he were a good deal younger, had just played the kind of schoolboy prank that occasionally amused him: This was the only time in eight years that he had been able to give the slip to the Secret Service. Often Mr. Truman acted on impulse, and he had just decided that he did not want bodyguards with him on this particular occasion. Perhaps guards would have slowed him down.

When the Vice-President emerged into the sunlight of Capitol Plaza, his waiting chauffeur, Tom Harty, barely had time to open the car door for his boss. Harty had often noticed that Mr. Truman did not particularly like to have such small services done for him. Then, Harty noticed the absence of Secret Servicemen; the Vice-President remarked that they would not be along.

A few moments earlier, while Mr. Truman was in Congressman Sam Rayburn's office, Steve Early, the Presidential

Secretary, telephoned: "Please come right over, quickly and quietly, and come in through the main Pennsylvania Avenue entrance."

Mr. Truman said a hasty good-by to Mr. Rayburn. Instead of going back to his office, where his guards waited for him, Mr. Truman took the elevator directly to the basement on the House side of the Capitol, then ran to the Senate side.

Now, as he impatiently rode through Washington's rush-hour traffic on Pennsylvania Avenue, Harry Truman knew little more than his chauffeur what he would find at the end of the trip.

This was April 12, 1945. At 5:25 P.M. Mr. Truman was ushered into a second-floor study at the White House. Eleanor Roosevelt told him the word she had just received:

"Harry, the President is dead."

At 7:09 P.M., by the clock beneath Woodrow Wilson's portrait in the Cabinet Room, the Vice-President took a Bible in his hand and repeated the Presidential Oath of Office after Chief Justice Harlan Stone:

"I, Harry S. Truman, do solemnly swear that I will faithfully execute the office of President of the United States, and will to the best of my ability, preserve, protect and defend the Constitution of the United States."

Members of the Cabinet had come to the White House to see the oath administered and, immediately following the ceremony, the new President held his first Cabinet meeting. Mr. Truman said he would try to continue the foreign and domestic policies of the Roosevelt Administration. He asked the members of the Cabinet to stay on, but he emphasized that he himself "would assume full responsibility for such decisions as had to be made."

The meeting lasted but a few moments, and then an era ended as the Roosevelt appointees filed out of the room. Among them were Harold Ickes . . . Henry Wallace . . . Henry Morgenthau . . .

One man—the oldest of them all—was slower to depart. Henry L. Stimson's fine white hair shone in the subdued light of the room, and his voice was a little unsteady as he said to the President there was something he had to tell him—without delay.

In a few hours Harry Truman would be telling his friends in the press just how the Presidency felt, as it fell suddenly on his shoulders: "Pray for me, boys; the moon, the stars and all the planets fell on me . . ."; but on that night of April 12 Secretary of War Stimson knew better than anyone else in the White House just how heavy Truman's responsibilities were to be. Stimson knew a secret that had been kept from the Vice-President.

In Mr. Truman's own words:

> *That first meeting of the Cabinet was short, and when it adjourned, the members rose and silently made their way from the room—except for Secretary Stimson.*
>
> *He asked to speak to me about a most urgent matter. Stimson told me that he wanted me to know about an immense project that was under way—a project looking to the development of a new explosive of almost unbelievable destructive power. That was all he felt free to say at the time, and his statement left me puzzled. It was the first bit of information that had come to me about the atomic bomb, but he gave me no details. It was not until the next day that I was told enough to give me some understanding of the*

> *almost incredible developments that were under way and the awful power that might soon be placed in our hands. That so vast an enterprise had been successfully kept secret even from the members of Congress was a miracle.*

So Stimson was the bearer of the second shocking surprise of the day. In Stimson's words: "Within four months we shall have completed the most terrible weapon ever known in all human history."

That night of April 12, various threads of history were already spinning into a pattern, making a new design for human life, beginning an era that men would call the Atomic Age.

At a secret laboratory, men of talent and genius were making the final calculations for "The Bomb." They were certain their new kind of bomb would work. Prominent scientists in charge of this project had been sure of that since December.

On secret practice flights from an airfield in Utah, Air Corps bombardiers for months had been preparing "The Plane" which could carry a secret new device. At this hour the crew and the ship were alert and ready. Whenever the device was completed, tested, and delivered to them, a single word could launch their mission.

In several secret groups, several spies working for the Soviet apparatus had already been assigned to espionage in nuclear energy. To a great extent, these agents were successful in learning of the atomic project in 1944 and 1945.

Mr. Truman was not aware of the magnitude and the importance of these threads of history, on this night of April

12. And of the dark web of espionage he and we did not learn until years later.

We will look from time to time at these other parts of the pattern of this history—the threads which give background to the dominant theme in which the President learned of a new weapon and faced the questions involved in its use.

When Tom Harty, and the Secret Servicemen who had rejoined Mr. Truman, drove with him up Connecticut Avenue to his apartment, a good part of the world had experienced one grave shock: *Franklin D. Roosevelt was dead.* Only a very few men knew of another shock to come: *a new age would be born.* These few were already thinking this new President would make a decision in about 100 days. This is the story of those days and that decision.

. . . It has been made probable through the work of Joliot in France, as well as Fermi and Szilard in America . . . that it may become possible to set up a nuclear chain reaction in a large mass of uranium . . .

. . . This new phenomenon would also lead to the construction of bombs . . . extremely powerful bombs . . .

—Albert Einstein to President Roosevelt, August 2, 1939

2.

"The Moon, the Stars and All the Planets"

THE CIVILIZED WORLD in April, 1945, was concerned with one main fact: *war.*

In the United States, mobilization was at the crest, with eleven million men under arms, and many millions more working in war industry. Less than a year before, the Allies had landed in Normandy.

Less than a month before, our Third Army had come across a wonderful lucky break: the bridge at Remagen. General Patton of the Third Army, engaged in successful pursuit of the Nazis, had assumed that the bridge across the Rhine at Remagen would have been blown up. It was not. Soon four divisions had poured across the river into Germany. Fifty thousand Germans were taken prisoner in one operation and now, by the middle of April, final victory in Europe was a matter of days.

Americans were already beginning to have a foretaste of triumph—and forebodings about the devastated world for which they shared responsibility.

Compared with our isolation of a few years before, we had a much larger view of the world in which man lives.

On our maps we had placed the names of Corregidor, Guadalcanal, Leyte, and the Coral Sea. By April, 1945, we had long since gone through Casablanca, and we had numbered some of the hills of Africa, such as Hill 609 near Kasserine Pass. Since then we had known Sicily, Anzio, Cassino, Omaha Beach, the hedgerows of Saint-Lô, and a great many other place names of power and tragedy.

But in the spring of 1945 very few men knew that the entire globe would soon be familiar with other new and still-secret names, the first colonies of a new world. A very few men had put upon their maps the names of Oak Ridge, Los Alamos, and Hanford. These were the secret atomic cities developing the basic fuel and the balance of world power for tomorrow.

The new President of the United States had not been one of the few officials admitted behind the atomic curtain. As Vice-President, Truman had no hint of the developments which nuclear physicists believed would be as important as the current war. The Manhattan Project and its purpose had never been a subject for any Cabinet discussions, although, for special reasons, a few Cabinet members had been told something of it. Most high government officials were equally in the dark about the fission of the atom or the manufacture of bombs.

At this time 100,000 persons were employed by the agencies or the contractors of the Manhattan Engineer District, the official name of the Project. Most of the workers had no idea what they were making on the ridge in Tennessee, or on the beautiful mesa at Los Alamos in New Mexico.

Yet, many British leaders knew about the secret project. Winston Churchill had taken pains to see that even His Majesty's Loyal Opposition, headed by Clement Attlee, was aware of the general hope for nuclear energy. During the war the Project was supposed to be a joint enterprise between the British and the Americans. However, Churchill often complained that the British were not being properly informed. The terms of the secret agreement between Roosevelt and Churchill had already caused great dissension between the Allies. Later the agreement was to cause even more trouble. It had been a kind of treaty—*but it had been kept secret from the Senate!*

In the war years no official word of the Project ever went to our other allies. Most surprising of all, many American military leaders were kept in the dark. Progress toward an A-bomb was not a subject for discussion by the Joint Chiefs of Staff, as far as one may learn from the notes they kept.

Key military people, General Douglas MacArthur for example, were not briefed to expect any special weapon. Nor was General Dwight D. Eisenhower told to expect a super-weapon soon. These men were sometimes disturbed by reports from their intelligence officers of weird new enemy weapons, such as the Germans' V-2. Yet, they were not told of our own secret weapon.

Within the Pentagon, Secretary of the Navy James Forrestal knew of the Project; but even in his secret diary, which was kept locked under security conditions, he would scarcely refer to it. For example, he would enter a note, without even using a capital letter, about a committee on "manhattan." It was as if in his diary he would not even mention the secret to himself.

Admiral William D. Leahy, the White House military and diplomatic adviser to FDR, was informed of the Project, but to the very last simply did not believe that any such tremendous explosive would prove to be practical. As a lifelong student of explosives, Leahy had good reason to have great confidence in his own judgment.

Later Navy spokesmen would complain that the Navy had really been neglected in not being told about this development. Yet in the very beginning physicists had approached the Navy with the idea of nuclear energy, and the Navy, in the words of the Smyth Report, "had expressed interest and asked to be kept informed." Years later, Navy officers were resentful of the manner in which "the Army had kept the secret from its ally, the Navy."

Henry L. Stimson, as Secretary of War, had been informed and for years had taken particular interest in the Project. To him had fallen the peculiar responsibility of seeing to it that men were not drafted away from essential atomic work into the Army. Some 50,000 persons were deferred from the Draft and assigned to the Project, but no draft board was ever told the nature of this essential work.

Perhaps the major support which the Army high command gave Brigadier General Leslie R. Groves, Director of the Project, was in assuring him of the men to do the job. In all other respects General Groves directed a peculiar Army project: the high command did not tell him what they wanted; he told them what he wanted. More peculiar still, he was responsible for spending hundreds of millions of dollars, approaching the two-billion mark, and not a single ounce of final product had ever been shipped from any of his production centers.

It was this peculiarity—*the production of nothing*—that had almost resulted in a premature disclosure of the secret mission of the Manhattan Project. Many months before he became President, Truman had come almost as close to the atomic secrets as he was on the fateful night of April 12. In both cases the person he finally came face to face with was Henry Stimson.

All appropriations for the Manhattan District, and these were running into the hundreds of millions, had passed through the hands of Congress, since no government agency receives money to spend in any way other than through specific acts of Congress. In this case, as in some others, Congress was asked for a blank check. And with this particular check, not only was the amount unknown, but also the payee and the purpose.

Naturally there were many secret projects during the war and, even when they were not secret, the very size of the wartime enterprise made it difficult for Congress to keep watch over expenditures. (This has been and still is a serious problem in a democracy. How can the public approve or disapprove of a government's policies and actions if it does not even know what the government has done or what it plans to do?)

Both the Senate and the House have committees for the special purpose of following military affairs; but even as the defense program grew to enormous size in 1939 and 1940, a Senator from Missouri was thinking that there should be a special Senate Committee for the particular purpose of investigating wartime contracts.

Senator Harry S. Truman introduced the resolution on February 10, 1940, which established the Committee to Investigate the National Defense Program. He became its Chairman and it became popularly known as the Truman Committee, even before we entered the war.

In 1944 the Truman Committee heard rumors of huge Army production centers which were consuming tons of vital materials. Entire trainloads of scarce construction materials, steel, copper, and cement, went into these places, and nothing ever came out.

There was such a place in New Mexico, near Albuquerque, and it happened that Senator Carl Hatch, from that state, had been assigned to the Truman Committee. There was also a place in Washington State, which was using up as much concrete as a giant dam and, by further coincidence, Senator Mon Wallgren of Washington was on the Truman Committee.

In Tennessee, men were building a place called K-25, which was to be the largest single industrial process under one roof anywhere in the world. But in 1944 this huge plant apparently produced nothing, and also appeared to be connected with these other far-flung projects of the Army Engineers Corps, of which Truman Committee Senators had personal knowledge.

Could this be the largest scandal of the war? (Inside the wall of secrecy, General Groves had once said, "If we succeed, they won't investigate us at all; if we fail, Congress for a long time won't investigate anything else.")

The accidents of history threatened to lead to an investigation of the Project before it could be finished. The investigators of the Truman Committee had already worked their way into Oak Ridge, the Tennessee site, when the probe was stopped by the word of one man: Truman called the investigation off after one short face-to-face session with Stimson.

In his own later words Truman said:

> I had even sent investigators into Tennessee and the state of Washington with instructions to find out what certain enormous constructions were and what their purpose was.
>
> At that time, when these investigators were sent out, Secretary Stimson had phoned me to say that he wanted to have a private talk with me. I told him that I would come to his office at once, but he said he would rather come to see me.

Who were these "investigators"? Truman's memoirs mention only one, an old personal friend. Many years before, Senator Truman had been responsible for making plans for a new courthouse in Jackson County, Missouri. This project fascinated Truman, and he took an automobile trip around America to see outstanding courthouses before he settled on a plan for his own. With him, as chauffeur and companion for 24,000 miles, Truman took a man named Fred Canfil. Later, Jonathan Daniels, a member of FDR's and Truman's White House staff, described Canfil as "a short, ugly man with the personality of a baited bear, but with a primitive bearlike loyalty." Through the years Canfil had been loyal and close to Truman, and it was he who had worked his way into Oak Ridge. But his determination was in vain. To return to Mr. Truman's account of the call from Mr. Stimson:

> As soon as he arrived, I learned that the subject he had in mind was connected with the immense installations I had sent the committee representatives to investigate in Tennessee and the state of Washington.
>
> "Senator," the Secretary told me as he sat beside my desk, "I can't tell you what it is, but it is the greatest project in the history of the world. It is most top secret. Many of the people who are actually engaged in the work have no idea what it is, and we who do would appreciate your not going into those plants."
>
> I had long known Henry L. Stimson to be a great American patriot and statesman.
>
> "I'll take you at your word," I told him. "I'll order the investigations into those plants called off."
>
> I did so at once, and I was not to learn anything whatever as to what that secret was until the Secretary spoke to me after that first Cabinet meeting.

Of course Mr. Stimson had only a few hurried moments to urge the new President to look into this matter as soon as possible. It would have taken hours for any man to describe the scope and the purpose of the secret atomic empire.

More than 100,000 persons and two billion dollars had built one secret laboratory after another, followed by fantastic production units.

First, at Columbia University, there had been a laboratory called SAM. Then there was another headquarters in Chicago, and part of that laboratory was beneath the stands of a football field. Chancellor Robert M. Hutchins had abolished football at the University of Chicago, and many people thought it was a shame to see that huge empty pile of concrete—more or less unused. But it *was* being used, and the first sustained chain reaction was brought in at Stagg Field.

At Oak Ridge, Tennessee, near a place called Happy Valley, men like Arthur Compton, Harold Urey, and Eugene Wigner had guided the construction of giant plants for the main purpose of separating one form of uranium, U-235, from another, U-238. Oak Ridge was then commonly known as "Dogpatch," but it had grown to be a city of 78,000 persons. Today any high school physics student knows that natural uranium contains both of the important isotopes, but that U-235 is the vital ingredient for maintaining a chain reaction.

At Oak Ridge, the Manhattan Project had built the largest industrial plants in the world devoted to a single process. Such plants combined huge size with extreme delicacy of operation. The purpose at K-25, as the gaseous-diffusion plant was called, was to work with uranium in a gaseous form. This gas was one of the most unpleasant things man had ever imagined, much less manufactured. To begin with, gaseous uranium hexafluoride is deadly *poisonous* and corrosive. And it is radioactive!

The method of separating the lighter uranium from the heavier is to pump the gas through many, many miles of pipe and chambers, constantly forcing it through very fine screens. The heavier gas molecules, containing U-238, tend, ever so slightly, to go through the screens at a slower speed than the lighter molecules. After going through a myriad of such barriers, there was more of the gas fraction carrying U-235. The process is simple in principle.

But the technology inside was quite involved! For example: the billions of holes in these barriers were each about one-millionth of an inch in diameter and, because uranium hexafluoride is corrosive, the barriers and holes had to be a special nickel alloy. These holes were nickel-plated!

At Hanford, Washington, they had spent a half-billion on huge machines to manufacture an element which Nature had not made, but man could make: plutonium. These machines, nuclear reactors, were heat-and-power plants on a huge scale, and the waters of the Columbia River were used to cool them. As a result the temperature of the river was noticeably raised.

There was a crisis one day when an official began a conference with one word: "Fish!" All present realized instantly that he was on a topic which had already worried some of them. The water in the Columbia River could not only be hot in terms of temperature; it could be made "hot" in terms of radiation. Safety measures were established, but radiation remained a serious problem at Hanford. Never before had man built such great equipment, knowing that once it was in operation, no men for centuries could ever again approach the hot, hot metal to make repairs. The Curse of King Tut's Tomb was a legend; this was real. Time and again the workmen at Hanford sealed off a secret chamber. And sometimes when a chamber was sealed, it must remain sealed until it was as old as the pyramids. Stalin and Einstein would be like names ancient to us as Julius Caesar, before men would knowingly handle certain of these things.

Hidden away in the desert of New Mexico was Los Alamos, the principal laboratory where theoreticians and experimentalists could propose new concepts and test them out. Los Alamos was then one of the finest laboratories in the world. But, militarily speaking, the primary role of the laboratory was as an ordnance center, the final point of assembly of the bomb from materials produced in Washington State and in Tennessee. The basic task for Los Alamos had been stated several years before by a Committee of the National Academy of Sciences (in October, 1941): "A fission bomb of superlatively destructive power will result from bringing quickly together a sufficient mass of U-235."

Oak Ridge had solved the problem of "sufficient mass." Los Alamos was now solving the problem of *"bringing quickly together."* The final calculations on this were being made, although scientists were confident that the basic solutions were at hand. However, they were quite anxious to see just how efficient the bomb would actually be in terms of released energy. Soon they would know. . . .

Henry Stimson had just visited Oak Ridge, in the first days of April.

That night of April 12 he thought both of the death at Warm Springs, Ga., and of the new life being born in Tennessee, in Washington, and in New Mexico.

A few minutes after Stimson had spoken to him about the Bomb Project, Harry Truman, as President, was home at his apartment on Connecticut Avenue.

Mrs. Truman and their daughter Margaret had been at the White House for the swearing-in ceremony, but had left when he went into the short Cabinet meeting. When the new President arrived at the family apartment, about 10:00 P.M., he did not find his wife and daughter at home. Correctly guessing that they were at the apartment next door, Mr. Truman went down the hall to find them, and to get something to eat. He had had nothing since lunch, ten hours before.

Vice-President and Mrs. Truman had been quite friendly with their next-door neighbors, General and Mrs. Jeff Davis, and the Davises fortunately had enjoyed a ham and turkey dinner that evening. So the new President's first meal was left-overs, "borrowed" from the neighbors. He ate heartily, returned immediately to his apartment, and went to bed and to sleep.

At 6:30 A.M., on April 13, he awoke, took his customary walk and had breakfast. It was to be his first day in office, but he could not know how full a day it would be.

At 9:00 A.M. he went downstairs to the White House car and found Hugh Fulton, the counsel for the Truman Committee, and a squad of Secret Servicemen waiting for him.

As he entered the car, he noticed Tony Vaccaro, an Associated Press reporter who had covered his activities as Vice-President. Mr. Truman invited Vaccaro to hop in, and the three men rode to the White House together.

Getting to work that morning was difficult for Mr. Truman, not only for emotional reasons, but simply as a matter of organization.

In the oval office which Presidents use, Roosevelt's official and personal belongings were everywhere. Ship models and ship prints were especially obvious, and Truman has written how terrible it seemed to change things around in a room so recently occupied by his predecessor. This morning he could not bring himself to touch any of the mementoes, but merely cleared a working space on the desk.

The new President was also anxious to avoid any interference with FDR's personal staff. These men, shocked and grief-stricken, were overwhelmed with duties in connection with the plans for the funeral.

Mr. Truman had no staff of his own, and in the confusion he was hardly able to find his way around the place, or to find someone to take a letter or answer a phone. On that first morning he had to call in William D. Simmons, who had been the executive office receptionist for years. Simmons took on some of the duties of a secretary, answering phone calls, and greeting many of the new President's callers.

One of the callers was a man who had narrowly missed being President himself. He was also one of the few men who knew that the White House would shortly have to decide whether or not to use the most terrible weapon in history.

It was 2:30 P.M., and Roosevelt had been dead less than twenty-four hours, when Simmons showed James F. Byrnes into the oval office. It was an emotional moment for both, when Byrnes met Harry Truman sitting in the Presidential chair that Byrnes might have had.

James F. Byrnes had had a truly extraordinary political career. Few men in American history have held such high posts in all three branches of the government: legislative, judicial, and executive.

Byrnes, an expert stenographer as well as lawyer, was at the turn of the twentieth century an official court reporter in his home state, South Carolina. He was always interested in politics, and in 1911 campaigned successfully for election to Congress. He was re-elected three times and in 1931 was elected to the Senate, serving ten years there. So Byrnes had been on the national stage of politics about thirty years longer than Truman, and in recent years had often been mentioned as a likely candidate for the White House. Roosevelt's campaign for a third term had dashed his hopes for that final prize.

When Roosevelt appointed him a Justice of the Supreme Court, Byrnes thought he had said good-by to politics forever. Yet, Byrnes left the Court in the impetuous way characteristic of him when, after only a few months' service on the Supreme Court, he heard the news of Pearl Harbor. Like many other Americans, the Justice felt his current job did not contribute in any immediate way to the war effort.

A few days after Pearl Harbor, Byrnes went to see FDR, as he often did, very early in the morning. Roosevelt was still in bed, but had been awake for hours, reading dispatches and memos. He gave Byrnes secret information which the public would not have for months, about the extent of damage of Japan's surprise bombing. This shocking disclosure blasted Byrnes out of the marble halls of the Supreme Court.

The President gave Byrnes a special unpublicized job of coordinating war legislation, and smoothing out differences between recommendations by the Executive and action by Congress. It was a peculiar job for a Supreme Court Justice, but one well suited to Byrnes' background in Congress and his ability at political maneuvering.

A few months later a super war agency was created, the Office of Economic Stabilization. The President called Byrnes to his bedside for an early-morning talk and urged him to take the post of Director of the O.E.S. Within an hour Byrnes said good-by to the Court.

In May of 1943 he became head of another super-agency, the Office of War Mobilization. In this job he had an office in the White House itself and virtually ran the domestic economic affairs of the country while FDR and others managed military and foreign policy. In this spot he was termed "the Assistant President."

In the early months of 1945 the President surprised him with an exceptional introduction into the field of foreign affairs; Roosevelt took Byrnes to the fateful Yalta conference of the Big Three—Churchill, Stalin, and FDR.

FDR also told him about the atomic project.

Strangely, as it may seem to us now, Mr. Byrnes later could not remember when that conversation took place. "I do not remember just when it was that President Roosevelt told me. . . . It was a hot summer afternoon and the two of us were sitting alone in his oval office. . . . Suddenly, and for no apparent reason, he began to tell me the awesome story . . ."

Mr. Byrnes' best recollection is that it was the summer of 1943, and at the time the President thought the Germans were ahead of us in the race to make a uranium bomb.

"After the first discussion," Mr. Byrnes reported, "neither the President nor I mentioned the project to each other for many months. In fact, no one ever talked about it unless it was absolutely necessary. I remember once mentioning it to Stimson . . . his reaction indicated surprise that I even knew about it."

A few months before Roosevelt's death, Byrnes was told that the scientists would know by April 1 whether or not the bomb would work. They would not have tested it by then, but their calculations would enable them to give a yes or a no to the War Department. As we shall see, Byrnes apparently did not receive all the progress reports from the Manhattan Project.

When he went to see the new President on April 12, Byrnes believed that the April 1 deadline had come and gone and that the Project was still in doubt. Byrnes was again a private citizen and these responsibilities were somewhat remote; he did not realize that the atomic decision was closer than he had previously been told.

Just five days before this appointment, Byrnes had resigned from the War Mobilization Office. On the day of Roosevelt's death he had been relaxing and enjoying his new-found privacy in his home at Spartanburg, South Carolina. James Forrestal, the Secretary of the Navy, telephoned him about Roosevelt's death and sent a plane to bring him to the capital.

Thus, as Truman put it, "I found out Jimmie was at the Shoreham and asked him to come over." Truman had two vitally important subjects he wanted to talk over with Byrnes. One concerned the many important state secrets Truman knew he had not been told. For example, the hottest secret Truman could think of was: What had really happened at Yalta? The Yalta Conference had been the subject of many recriminations by the Republicans, and very little of the inside story had leaked to the press. Even within official circles the story was not too clear, for, generally speaking, the records of the Yalta meeting were not the usual transcripts made of such high-level conferences.

Mr. Truman remembered that the *ex-stenographer* Jimmie Byrnes had made a great many personal shorthand notes at Yalta. When he requested them, Byrnes readily agreed to transcribe these notes and send them to the White House; they arrived ten days later.

The other subject Truman wanted to discuss with Byrnes was a real surprise. Stunned though he was by the rush of events, Truman had already given thought to the problem of the Presidential succession: as President, Truman would have no Vice-President. The law provided that the Secretary of State succeed him, should Truman die or be incapacitated.

Truman and Byrnes talked over the fact that Edward R. Stettinius, Jr., who was then Secretary of State, had never been elected to any office by the American voters. He was a capable man, and no disrespect was meant toward him, but if anything were to happen to Truman, "President Stettinius" would sound even more strange to the public than the "President Truman" whom Americans were at that moment trying to accept.

Truman then made the surprising suggestion that Byrnes might be his Secretary of State; this, despite the fact that he and Byrnes had never been close friends. They had brushed somewhat unpleasantly against each other for years. Even when the still-unknown Senator from Missouri had been starting out with his Truman Committee and had asked for twenty-five thousand dollars for committee funds, the famous Mr. Byrnes, well known for his economy and then Chairman of the Committee on Audit and Control, was responsible for cutting that amount to ten thousand dollars. Later, they had far more reason to feel cool toward each other.

It is not in the nature of things that a man who is Vice-President is going to get along very well with a man who is called "Assistant President." Perhaps more important, they had been political rivals, leading contenders for the greatest prize of all.

Truman has written that he asked Byrnes to be his Secretary of State both because he was a capable man, and because Truman thought it might heal some of the bitterness between them. Byrnes accepted, but said he could not take office for some weeks. Meanwhile, Secretary Stettinius would continue to represent United States foreign policy, notably in preparing and attending the forthcoming San Francisco Conference, which would organize the United Nations.

Byrnes then spoke to Truman about the atom. One might think that this discussion would have been a long one. A President and his future Secretary of State might well have talked about the effect that atomic fission would have upon our foreign policy and our strength as a great power. Yet, Byrnes does not even mention this conversation in his own memoirs, and Truman gives it only a few lines in his. Truman reported that Byrnes, "with great solemnity, said that we were perfecting an explosive to destroy the whole world." Byrnes thought "the bomb might well put us in a position to dictate our own terms at the end of the war."

President Truman did not again see Secretary Stimson until twelve days later, and he was not at this time equipped to ask Mr. Byrnes questions. Byrnes, for that matter, could not have given him many details. They had many other things to talk about, and on that hectic day there were probably fifty things they might have mentioned if their foresight had been as good as human hindsight.

One of their omissions is particularly ironic: It did not occur to either of them that news of the impending atomic bomb might be given to Stettinius, who was still Secretary of State. No one had told Stettinius about the thing Navy Secretary Forrestal called "manhattan." Nor did they tell other members of our first UN delegation—men like Harold E. Stassen and John Foster Dulles.

In later years these delegates were angry about this omission. These men, on April 25, had gone to San Francisco as principal architects of the United Nations, but no one in our delegation knew that the power structure of the world would soon be changed.

In the course of this history, many men walked close to the door marked SECRET, but by design or luck were not called to the knowledge and responsibility of the first bomb. This list includes Eisenhower, MacArthur, Stassen, and Dulles, and, to some extent, the entire State Department until the time Byrnes became Secretary.

Later Mr. Stettinius was to realize that for weeks in the spring and summer of 1945 he was, as the saying goes, just one heartbeat away from the Presidency. If that heart had failed, Mr. Stettinius, too, would have found that there had fallen on him, the sun, the moon . . . and the atomic bomb.

"When we were in San Francisco in the spring of 1945,"

Secretary of State Dulles has said, "none of us knew of the atomic bomb which was to fall on Hiroshima on August 6, 1945. The Charter is thus a pre-atomic age charter. In this sense it was obsolete before it actually came into force. As one who was at San Francisco, I can say with confidence that if the delegates there had known that the mysterious and immeasurable power of the atom would be available as a means of mass destruction, the provisions of the Charter dealing with disarmament and the regulation of armaments would have been far more emphatic and realistic."

Mr. Dulles spoke "with confidence" in 1953, when he made this speech. But who can say whether the agreements would have been quite different? Not all the delegations were so ignorant of the atom as ours. The British were informed, and who can now say that the Russians were not?

3.

"manhattan"

> "I felt as if I had lived five lifetimes in my first five days as President."
>
> —Harry S. Truman

PRESIDENT ROOSEVELT had died at 3:55 P.M., on April 12. That was Thursday and the funeral was set for Sunday.

While the nation—and the world—mourned, the new President had far more work to do than the average President in peacetime. Perhaps the world was never busier.

First day, April 12

That Thursday, even before he had taken the oath of office Truman had been reminded that plans called for the opening conference of the United Nations, to be held in San Francisco, on April 25, less than two weeks away. After a few moments' thought, Truman decided that the opening of the conference should not be delayed because of Roosevelt's death. The UN's first meeting was discussed at the emergency Cabinet meeting, and following that, President

Truman had his previously mentioned short conversation with Secretary Stimson.

In the preceding chapter we have already glimpsed the interview with Byrnes, at which the bomb was briefly mentioned. It may be useful to note some of the other events of that second day of his presidency—and of the other early days.

Second day, April 13

In the morning his first caller was Secretary of State Stettinius, who told him further of plans for the United Nations meeting, and reviewed the current foreign policy. Truman asked that a complete list of the principal problems with other countries be prepared for him that same day. This was done and that night the new President read it. The report devoted to the Soviet Union began, "Since the Yalta conference, the Soviet government has taken a firm and uncompromising position on nearly every major question . . ."

At 11:00 A.M. that Friday, Secretary Stimson, Secretary Forrestal, General Marshall, Admiral Leahy, and others came to a meeting on the military situation. They told Truman that Germany would not be overcome for another six months at least, and Japan would not be conquered for another year and a half. The atom was not mentioned, although all of these men knew of "manhattan."

That noon the President drove to the Capitol to lunch with such Congressional leaders as Senators Alben Barkley and Arthur Vandenberg. Truman asked them to arrange a joint session of the Senate and the House so that he might address them in person.

In those first few hours President Truman also made a special point of inviting Prime Minister Churchill to fly to the United States to attend Roosevelt's funeral. Truman's hope was that, after the funeral, Churchill and he might have two or three days' talk. Churchill went so far as to order a plane readied, but was then persuaded that he must stay in England for certain important affairs, in particular the conduct of important debates in Parliament.

Later Churchill was to write of this decision.

> In the after-light I regret that I did not adopt the new President's suggestion. I had never met him . . . It seemed to me extraordinary, especially during the last few months, that Roosevelt had not made his deputy and potential successor thoroughly acquainted with the whole story and brought him into the decisions which were being taken. This proved of grave disadvantage to our affairs. There is no comparison between reading about events afterwards and living through them from hour to hour.

In the afternoon of that second day, after Byrnes mentioned the bomb during his visit, Secretary of State Stettinius called again, now accompanied by Charles Bohlen. The three men plunged into the difficult question of the troubles the Allies were having with the Soviet over Poland. Truman had always been a heavy reader, but he has said, "On that first full day as President I did more reading than I ever thought I could."

Third & Fourth days, April 14 and 15

On Saturday Mr. Truman arose earlier than usual. Since he was ordinarily an early riser, this meant that he was awake at dawn. Before breakfast he made some notes on the speech he planned to make before Congress on Monday.

Henry Wallace and James Byrnes met him at his office and the three went to meet the Roosevelt funeral train. By 11:30 A.M. Truman and other officials had escorted the flag-draped casket to the East Room and the President had returned to his office.

One of his appointments was with Harry Hopkins, who had been Roosevelt's closest personal adviser. The two men talked for two hours without even taking time out for luncheon; they ordered a tray from the White House kitchen and had a bite or two while they went over the entire range of world affairs and world personalities.

In the afternoon Admiral Leahy came in with a message from Churchill concerning a project that Roosevelt had proposed just two weeks before: The Chiefs of Staff had suggested the idea of taking obsolete bombers, loading them with huge cargoes of explosives, and sending them off toward industrial targets in Germany. These bombers, guided by remote control, would not return.

Churchill was not in favor of the plan, because the Germans might retaliate with similar blind robot-bombers against London, and "even a few very big explosions in London would be demoralizing to the people at a time when they hoped that their prolonged ordeal was over."

Mr. Truman thought this over and replied to Churchill that the idea should be dropped.

The war situation in the Pacific also made demands on the President's attention. The military were preparing a Pacific operation under the code name CORONET. This enterprise was planned to be larger even than OVERLORD, the code name given to the D-day offensive launched in Normandy.

That Saturday night the President and many Cabinet officials went by special train to Hyde Park for the final burial ceremony for Mr. Roosevelt.

Fifth day, April 15

On Monday morning the President and the country started a new regime.

The President would have preferred to spend more time on his special message to Congress, but that morning he was again immersed in the Russian question. The Secretary of State brought messages from Churchill. Later Anthony Eden, the British Foreign Minister, and Lord Halifax, the British Ambassador, came to inform him further of British views. All of them were working on a joint statement from the President and the Prime Minister to Marshal Stalin. In that message they told the Marshal that it seemed to them that the Russians were going back on agreements made at Yalta.

Truman has said that he "was beginning to realize how little the Founding Fathers had been able to anticipate the preparations necessary for a man to become President . . . when one is forced to make it without warning . . ." In the eighty-two days that Truman had been Vice-President, Roosevelt had not been in Washington more than a month, and Truman had paid him only two official calls. Altogether, as a candidate for the Vice-Presidency, as Vice-President-elect, and as Vice-President, Truman saw FDR on only eight official occasions.

Those first busy days led Truman to write his mother

that he wondered if *any* past leader had seen so much happen so fast.

On April 17 Mr. Truman held his first press conference. The reporters asked him dozens of questions—about Russia, about the United Nations, about rumored changes in the Cabinet. They also wanted to know if he intended to lift the wartime ban against horse racing. (This ban was aimed neither at horse racing nor at bookies—but at automobiles in view of the scarcity of gasoline.)

On April 20 the President met with the Chairman of the American Zionists to review the position of the Jews, the Arabs, and the British on Palestine.

By way of relaxation Mr. Truman lunched with his brother Vivian and two other Missourians. One was Fred Canfil, the man who had gotten into Oak Ridge—briefly—before Senator Truman had called him out. By this time Canfil had been appointed a United States marshal for the Western District of Missouri.

On April 22 the Russian delegate to the United Nations meeting, Vyacheslav Molotov, stopped off in Washington to visit Truman. He received an exceptionally blunt talk, minus any diplomatic euphemisms, from the new President. It was so rough that Molotov said, "I have never been talked to like that in my life."

"Carry out your agreements and you won't get talked to like that," the President replied, according to his recollection as recorded in his memoirs.

On April 24 Stimson sent Truman another reminder about the atom:

Dear Mr. President, I think it very important that I should have a talk with you as soon as possible on a highly secret matter. I mentioned it to you shortly after you took office but have not urged it since on account of the pressures you have been under. It, however, has such a bearing on our present foreign relations and has such an effect upon all my thinking in this field that I think you ought to know about it without much further delay.

(*signed*)
HENRY L. STIMSON
Secretary of War

Knowing that Stimson was referring to "manhattan," Truman instructed his appointment secretary Matt Connelly to arrange for the Secretary to come in at noon the next day, April 25. It was just twelve days since Byrnes had mentioned the super-bomb. Truman knew that Stimson would have important policy matters to discuss; he did not yet know that Stimson regarded the bomb as much more than just another weapon.

Secretary Stimson brought with him General Leslie R. Groves, the wartime head of the Manhattan Project.

These three, who talked that morning in the sunlit oval office, were very different kinds of men. They had only one element common to their backgrounds. They had all been or were Army men; but their military careers had been as strikingly different as were their appearances.

General Groves had the beefy physique of a onetime football player, now approaching middle age. He was a hard-driving administrator who asked nothing of subordinates he did not ask of himself—and he worked almost around the clock.

The General had traveled tens of thousands of miles over the country since the start of the defense program. He had been in charge of the construction of millions of dollars' worth of Army barracks, and he had also been a key figure in the building of the Pentagon. That is how he had come to be picked for the atomic job which, in part, was a huge construction project.

General Groves was a West-Pointer, but far from the usual image of the man from the Point. He was not trim of figure, nor clipped in his speech, nor insistent on military punctilio. Deeply tanned, black-haired, and heavy-jowled, he looked and acted the big construction man.

Secretary Stimson, at seventy-seven, was quite the oldest of the three. Though very slightly stooped, he was also the tallest.

His father had been a Wall Street broker and, later, a surgeon. The young Stimson had attended Phillips Academy in Andover and Yale and Harvard for his law education. As a young New York lawyer Stimson had entered politics and soon became well known, notably as an adviser to Theodore Roosevelt. Stimson had already been a Cabinet officer, familiar with the White House for some years, before Harry Truman was a Captain of Artillery in World War I.

No one would have described Stimson in the words Truman once applied to himself: "I look like fifty people you saw on the street last week." He was the most handsome of the three, and the slight cragginess of his features only added to his commanding appearance. He gave the impression of being an old eagle—above most battles but one who would never shrink from any issue that had to be met.

As far as the atomic project was concerned, few men at that time had given it the earnest thought that Stimson had. He had prepared a searching memorandum, which he wanted to discuss with Truman. In presenting it, Stimson was having his first real conference with the new President, but he had been conferring with Presidents for forty years.

Stimson had also fought in the Army, as a Colonel in World War I. This morning the military rank of the three men was the reverse of their civilian rank. General Groves reported to the "Colonel," who was reporting to the "Captain."

The "Captain" regarded Secretary Stimson as a man of great wisdom and foresight, and listened with absorbed interest as the "Colonel" read from his prepared memo.

Just two days before Truman became President, Stimson had visited Oak Ridge, Tennessee, and his impressions were fresh in his mind. The news concerned a bomb equal in power to all the high explosives and artillery of both wars.

Stimson's memorandum of April 25 began:

> 1. Within four months we shall in all probability have completed the most terrible weapon ever known in human history, one bomb of which could destroy a whole city.
>
> 2. Although we have shared its development with the United Kingdom, physically the U. S. is at present in the position of controlling the resources with which to construct and use it and no other nation could reach this position for some years.
>
> 3. Nevertheless, it is practically certain that we could not remain in this position indefinitely.

With typical incisiveness, Stimson had come to the core question of atomic policy: How long could we expect to have any kind of monopoly of this weapon? On the answer to this would hinge much of our postwar policy.

The memorandum went on to state that "various segments of its discovery and production are widely known among many scientists in many countries. . . . It is extremely probable that the future will make it possible for atomic bombs to be constructed by smaller nations or even groups, or at least by a larger nation in a much shorter time."

Within a few months the American public was to hear conflicting views as to when or whether other countries would be able to build an atomic weapon. The military sources, including General Groves himself, consistently said it would be ten to twenty years, and some felt that for practical purposes "non-industrial countries like Russia" could not become atomic powers within the foreseeable future. However, scientists familiar with the technical problems and international science supported the judgment of Stimson, that "the future will make it possible for atomic bombs to be constructed by smaller nations or even groups . . . or by a larger nation in a much shorter time."

As Stimson read his memorandum that morning, some of the nightmare quality of the atomic world came into the discussion.

> . . . the future may see a time when such a weapon may be constructed in secret and used suddenly and effectively . . . by a wilful nation . . . against an unsuspecting nation. . . . with its aid, even a very powerful unsuspecting nation might be conquered with a very few days by a very much smaller one. . . .
>
> . . . the world in its present state of moral advancement compared with its technical development would be eventually

> at the mercy of such a weapon. In other words, modern civilization might be completely destroyed.

When James F. Byrnes had spoken with the President a few days before, he had emphasized the awesome power of the weapon. He had looked upon it mainly as a weapon, and what it could do to advance the national interest, if used in war. Byrnes, as Mr. Truman later put it, had said "in his belief the bomb might well put us in a position to dictate our own terms at the end of the war." But Stimson, the President said, "seemed at least as much concerned with the role of the atomic bomb in the shaping of history as in its capacity to shorten this war."

This very day the United Nations was meeting for the first time.

Stimson continued reading from his memo.

> To approach any world peace organization of any pattern now likely to be considered, without an appreciation by the leaders of our country of the power of this weapon, would seem to be unrealistic. No system of control heretofore considered would be adequate to control this menace. Both inside any particular country and between the nations of the world, the control of this weapon will undoubtedly be a matter of the greatest difficulty and would involve such thoroughgoing rights of inspection and internal controls as we have never heretofore contemplated.

By "system of control" Stimson did not mean the physical control of the chain reaction, although to the man in the street that became a real question: "Can man control atomic energy?" That question, to the average man, was similar to wondering whether man could someday control the weather. The average man feared that the reaction would "get out of hand" someday and rage like a hurricane around the world.

Stimson's fear was not of the physical atom but of political man.

In most disarmament proposals—and Stimson had spent years working for disarmament—it is a relatively simple matter for great powers to verify that an agreement is carried out. Nations may agree to limit their navies: Then, perhaps, one nation has to sink ships already built; another has to stop construction of ships on the way, etc. But these actions are easy to observe; to check on them requires no extensive "inspection system." The treaty nations can assure themselves that these ordinary weapons are being controlled and the agreements are being honored.

Atomic production, however, would be vastly different from ship construction. Stimson thought it might be tragically—even fatally—different. He did not, at this time, anticipate what an obstacle the matter of inspection would be to negotiating atomic control with the USSR; but he could imagine that Americans would not take warmly to the idea of foreign inspectors going through Oak Ridge, telling free Americans what they could or could not do, under a world agreement.

Soon, it would be possible to pack the power to destroy a city within a space the size of a man's suitcase. Establishing inspection against production of such weapons would involve, as Stimson put it, a kind of control such "as we have never heretofore contemplated."

Stimson also foresaw some of the main implications of atomic secrecy. This first memorandum on the bomb said:

> . . . the question of sharing it with other nations and, if so shared, upon what terms, becomes a primary question of our foreign relations. Also our leadership in the war and in the development of this weapon has placed a certain moral responsibility upon us which we cannot shirk without very serious responsibility for any disaster to civilization which it would further.
>
> . . . if the problem of the proper use of this weapon can be solved, we would have the opportunity to bring the world into a pattern in which the peace of the world and our civilization can be saved. . . .

From this discussion Truman got the impression that

> no one could positively know that the gigantic effort that was being made would be successful. . . . Nevertheless, the Secretary appeared confident of the outcome . . . within the next few months. . . . If expectations were to be realized . . . the atomic bomb would be certain to have a decisive influence on our relations with other countries . . . if it worked . . . in all probability, would shorten the war.

Stimson urged the President to appoint a group of men to consider atomic problems. Stimson said he himself had "already been planning to do so. . . . Steps are under way looking towards the establishment of a select committee of particular qualifications for recommending action to the executive and legislative branches of our government when secrecy is no longer in full effect . . ."

The President agreed to appoint such a committee. It was to be a highly secret group, known as the Interim Committee. Stimson was its Chairman and Truman's personal representative to the group was James F. Byrnes.

With general agreement on this step, the President concluded the meeting. He said later that he "thanked [Stimson] for his enlightening presentation . . . and as I saw him to the door I felt how fortunate the country was to have so able and so wise a man in its service."

4.

"A Single Plane"

THERE ARE DAYS in the life of man in which many waves of history seem to come to a crest and break. On this day of April 25 the streets of San Francisco were crowded with hundreds of men from all over the world, talking of peace in a hundred tongues, voicing the hopes and fears of millions. The eyes of the world turned toward peace as the first UN conference held its opening meeting.

In Italy, April 25 was the prearranged day on which the Italian underground would rise up behind the German lines. The Partisans rose with bloody violence and great success. As one result, a group found the hiding place of the Italian dictator and with mob spirit running high, the Partisans dragged Mussolini and Clara Petacci, his mistress, toward an ignominious death.

In Germany, April 25 was the day on which the Russian troops made their first entrance into the outskirts of Berlin, block by block. Just as the Germans had once scorched their way into Russian cities, the Russians now burned and blasted their way before them, house by house, against last-ditch Nazi resistance. The Russians knew it was only a matter of hours or days until they reached the center of the city.

In 1945 most men were watching these surface threads in the loom of history, not knowing that they were small compared with those which soon would appear: for example, the thread of action preparing one plane to carry one bomb on one mission.

During these last days of April, and even as Stimson spoke to Truman on April 25, a picked crew of airmen and bombardiers was making last-minute preparations for going overseas.

For many months the 509th Composite Group, stationed at Wendover Field, in a desert area of Utah, had been rehearsing the dropping of a special secret weapon. Now that these men had finished their training, they were hot to fly with the real thing.

But what was the real thing? These airmen knew of a few characteristics; they knew that some of the details were quite unpleasant; but only their commanding officer had been given even a sketchy briefing. And he had been forbidden to pass this briefing on to his men.

So the men of the 509th, like the President of the United States, knew very little about the weapon. They knew nothing of the secret cities of Oak Ridge and Los Alamos, and those cities knew nothing of the 509th.

However, there were a few men who did have both Oak Ridge and Wendover Field on their maps. These men were making a gamble and a judgment. They were gambling on a certain test. If that gamble came out all right, then they judged there might be orders to deliver a new weapon. If both the test and the decision said "yes," these men realized there had to be some Air Force men and some bombers that could make the delivery. That judgment was SOP, or Standard Operating Procedure. Nothing else about the 509th could be described as SOP, particularly not "the thing."

At Wendover Field, the GI's had given it a special name. They called it "The Gimmick."

About two years before, the original gamblers had decided to prepare completely for this mission, though it might never materialize.

There were a few generals charged with the conduct of the war who were also informed of "manhattan." One of them was the Army Air Force chief, General "Hap" Arnold, who had been briefed by General Groves. "Hap" Arnold immediately decided to have bombers ready. But what planes could do it?

By September of 1943 the B-29's, first of the famous Superforts, were coming off the production line and were chosen for the job. Designers and technicians began to modify the aircraft, to produce a special few with the ability to carry an outsize device of some kind in their bomb bays. However, it was said that "the modifications were substantial but not radical." It seems "The Gimmick" was to be tailored to fit the plane, rather than the plane to fit "The Gimmick."

In the summer of 1944, at about the time that FDR was telling the leaders of the Chicago Democratic convention that his choice for Vice-President was Truman and not Byrnes, General "Hap" Arnold was personally selecting a certain B-29 test pilot from Eglin Field as C.O. of a specially formed air group. The President and this pilot were to be the "first and last link" in a strange chain of command.

The new C.O., Colonel Paul W. Tibbets, Jr., was officially described as a superb pilot with a distinguished record. He had, indeed, a fine combat record with another pioneer group, the 97th Bombardment Group of North Africa and Europe. He was judged to have the knowledge of engineering, the abilities of leadership and skill as a pilot, and the bravery, required for this mission of unknown hazards.

He was given a high priority in gathering personnel for his outfit, because "the ultrasecret nature of the project and its potential importance called for personnel of the highest qualifications." Colonel Tibbets' B-29's were to be fairly typical and the core of the team was a typical B-29 squadron but, as an organization, there were many things different about the 509th.

For one thing, it was given a peculiar independence from the rest of the Army Air Forces. (Ground and air forces were part of the same service in World War II.) The 509th operated somewhat on its own, because the theory was that the more independence it had, the better the secrecy.

The name "Composite Group" indicated that various elements were gathered under one umbrella. Some were odd, indeed. They had a heavy Military Police detail, and on top of that was something called the First Ordnance Squadron (Aviation). The latter outfit would have guarded "The Gimmick," except that it wasn't there to guard. Later there was an even stranger detachment, which included professors. Several people in this unit had foreign accents, but even more alien to many army people was the presence of a naval officer, Captain W. S. Parsons.

This unit was called First Technical Detachment, War Department, Miscellaneous Group. No one was ever to hear of any Second Ordnance Squadron, or any Second Technical Detachment. Each was one of a kind.

Colonel Tibbets was a perfectionist. He personally selected bleak Wendover Field as a training base because he thought that, being located far out in the desert, it would be much simpler to maintain security. The Colonel trained his new crews intensively and "made a fetish" of perfect timing. If planes arrived from a long practice mission even five minutes late, it could make the Colonel angry.

By December of 1944 the ordinary SOP training of the crews was finished, and the young Colonel began introducing the men to special features peculiar to their group: Their planes had the depressing distinction of having all turrets and guns stripped off, except the twin .50-caliber fins in the tail. The stripping did nothing to raise the morale of the 509th. In any case, the B-29, as a plane, was not yet as popular as it later became with pilots. After experience with the B-19's and the B-24's, pilots found the new plane "hot to handle." The B-29's stalling speed was 125 miles an hour, and it required special flaps to enable it to land at any reasonable speed.

It had been decided from the beginning that the B-29's would not use radar in pinpointing the target, but would operate by the old-fashioned visual method, using human eyes and bombsights. The general opinion of men of the 509th was that the visual method was fine—on a clear day!

They did not know that great care would be taken to send them over on a clear day.

These special features, and others that came up later, set the group apart. Official history describes the separation as stemming from the "peculiar command arrangements, the partial geographical separation, the special aircraft insignia, rigid security measures, and the failure to participate in ordinary combat missions."

Perhaps secrecy was the main thing. Secrecy was always complete and this was bound to cause certain misadventures. A special overseas base area was being constructed in the Pacific for the 225 officers and 1542 men of the 509th. The location of the base was chosen because it was not too close to the main traffic ways of military aviation in the Pacific. Eventually the 509th's special area was to be an island within an island.

But there was one big hitch: The powers-that-be in the Pacific did not know of any reason to give "crash" priority to construction for this unknown and unproven group. Elmer E. Kirkpatrick, an engineer and Colonel with the Twentieth Air Force, had to fly out to the Pacific to pour on the heat. "Elmer the Expediter" deserves better than a footnote in history, for without him there would have been impossible delays in putting up shelter for laboratories and a storage place for "The Gimmick." Kirkpatrick got them off of dead center.

Toward the end of April the overseas base was finished and the 509th had completed training. On May 6 the first shipment of ground maintenance crews left Seattle in a troop ship. They did not, of course, know they were going to the Marianas—to the island of Tinian—where they would still be isolated from other military personnel while they waited for the orders to fly.

In these spring weeks, these crews knew none of what was to come. Neither did they know that "The Gimmick" had not even been tested and did not really "exist."

5.

"A Single Bomb"

A FEW HUNDRED MILES south of Wendover Field, Utah, another group of men was occupied with another rehearsal. These men, too, lived in a rough environment in the desert, but the landscape was beautiful. Their camp stood on a high tableland near a canyon where tall poplars pointed to the dry blue sky.

This camp was named for the poplars: Los Alamos. All around this remote mesa were places with beautiful Spanish names . . . Parajito Canyon, Espanola, the Sangre de Cristo Mountains, and the Jornada del Muerto—the area called the Journey of Death.

To reach this camp, one would go first to Albuquerque, New Mexico, and then to Santa Fe. The "site" was only two dozen miles from Santa Fe, but one could not travel directly. First one would drive north to an ancient Spanish-American village, Espanola. Then, one turned back—by a hairpin turn, as they say in the Southwest. The second leg of the road winds a tortuous way for sixteen miles along the tableland—it runs along at the edge of the table, so to speak. To the right of the road is the precipitous drop to the canyon. This spring of 1945, humanity walked a tightrope road beside this canyon.

Over this road, little more than a trail, there had traveled, in the two years past, a thousand trucks carrying strange instruments and thousands of men speaking a strange language. These men talked of thousands of tons of energy, as if energy had weight. They talked of thousandths and then of millionths of a second, as if with a very sharp knife they could slice time itself into transparent nothing.

Over this desert trail, in utmost secrecy, men brought the great Harvard cyclotron—they brought it in parts into the desert, and put it together again. They put it together faster than the construction men could raise a building around it, and then worked through many night *to tune the cyclotron.*

On the maps of the Army, and of the future, the place at the end of this sandy road was called Site Y.

In April of 1945 Site Y was approaching its crucial "test." For years the spirit of genius and the sweat of labor had gambled on this one ultimate trial. More than 100,000 men, at Site Y, X-10, K-25, and others, had spent some two billion dollars and fabricated a few pounds of silvery-looking metal. Here at Site Y only a few men had ever looked upon the dull silver of uranium, but the whole enterprise was dedicated to what could be done with it.

Site Y at that time was one of the world's greatest laboratories. It was managed by a slender young theoretician, an erudite professor who read Sanskrit for recreation and inspiration. This was J. Robert Oppenheimer. Around him were gathered some of the finest minds of what will surely be known as the Golden Age of Physics.

Just as conversation must have been continuous when Franklin, Jefferson, Hamilton, and Washington gathered in Philadelphia to start a new country, so conversation went on excitedly round the clock at Site Y, as men were starting a new world. In varied languages, a strange particle, the neutron, was being discussed by Enrico Fermi, Niels Bohr, Hans Bethe, Otto Frisch, James Chadwick, Ernest O. Lawrence, and other scientists from all over the world. Night after night they asked questions only an Einstein or your child will ask. "What is matter?" "How short can 'a short time' be?"

Los Alamos had the special mission of manufacturing a weapon. Here, in rough temporary buildings, men were learning the special nature of the chain reaction and studying the critical-mass problem.

One of the problems they discussed was like this: A lump of uranium below a certain size does not give off enough neutrons to cause an explosion. But a larger lump, of carefully determined size, will create an explosion. Up to 212° F., water does not boil. At 212° F. it boils. Loosely speaking, this is a sort of heat threshold. At Site Y they were looking for a certain neutron threshold that would be beyond the critical size.

Yet it was not that simple.

Suppose one took two lumps and brought them toward each other. Each is giving off a shower of neutrons. Thus as the lumps come closer to a collision, they shower each other with radiation, and they begin to disintegrate; they begin to crumble as would two lumps of sugar if they could bombard each other with rain.

This was the problem the scientists had stated years

before. How to get these sub-critical lumps together without disintegration but for an explosion? There would perhaps be no explosion if the lumps did not meet exactly as they should.

It had, thus, come down to a matter of timing! And at Site Y they feared they might not have an explosion but something more mild, like a melting in Hell's own April shower.

As one professor said, "It might be a mess. It might be a disaster. But it still would not be a bomb."

Another professor, from Princeton, was writing this spring of the crucial problem of these sub-critical pieces and the supreme need for speed in bringing them together. Dr. Henry Smyth said at this time:

> . . . the bomb must consist of a number of separate pieces each one of which is below the critical size either by reason of small size or unfavorable shape. . . . the problem, therefore, is two-fold: (1) to reduce the time of assembly to a minimum; and (2) to reduce the number of stray neutrons to a minimum.

Dr. Smyth and the others were talking about thousandths of seconds and thousands of pounds of TNT-equivalent.

To clarify the timing problem, they built strange kinds of guns in Parajito Canyon.

They were planning explosions which at first exploded inward, and then outward. The strange bullets in this gun were to be fired at each other, and, on impact, would devour one another. After the first, so-called, implosion there would be the grand explosion. They hoped.

Dr. Louis Slotin and others built this gunlike machine

to test some of these theoretical calculations. It worked rather simply and was not at all as impressive as a cyclotron.

A certain amount of uranium was placed in the grip of the machine. Perhaps that first test piece of uranium was shaped like a doughnut, and, from a tower above the first target piece, another piece of uranium was dropped through the hole in the doughnut. For a split second, the addition of the uranium passing through the hole would bring the whole assembly closer to the critical mass and size. This was the condition they wanted to measure. Apart from the extraordinarily delicate and difficult measurements, this was all there was to the test.

It was exciting to operate this thing and it did produce the needed facts. Sometimes they called this operation "twisting the dragon's tail." When the second lump of uranium dropped through the first, there would be an invisible spray of neutrons, imperceptible to the senses but recorded in the frantic dance of all the delicate instrument needles. Sometimes the needles "hit the ceiling"—they went "off-scale." Then the scientists could feel heat perceptible to the senses. One day, in fact, the device melted down the plastic which held certain parts in place. The operating crew learned something. This spring these men began to think of man-made temperatures as hot as the sun.

It was an ugly machine. They nicknamed it "The Guillotine."

Young Dr. Louis Slotin ran many radiation experiments on this instrument. He knew that many men might, one day, die of such radiation; he did not know that Louis Slotin would be one of them. It was merciful for Slotin, and, perhaps, for many of those at Los Alamos, that they could not read the future.

But many scientists spent many nights thinking about the revolution in which this ugly thing was The Guillotine, a blade between yesterday and tomorrow.

6.

An Interim — "A Long View of History"

IN THE BUSY DAYS following his April 25 conference with President Truman, Secretary Stimson collected a group to consider atomic policy and the weapon, called S-1. This was the Interim Committee, and some decisions of this group swayed history more than most American cabinets have done.

Stimson was Chairman, but he himself said, "the principal labor of guiding its extended deliberations fell to George L. Harrison, who acted as chairman in my absence . . ."

Truman named Byrnes to be the official representative of the White House. Byrnes was a private citizen at the time, and there is no record that there was any clearance procedure for him before he was granted further access to the greatest secrets the nation then possessed. (This procedure was not unusual for high officials in the pre-atomic age. Mr. Byrnes was "known to be a good citizen." This was long before we reached the era when prospective Secretaries of State would be checked by the FBI.)

All other members of the committee were officials:

Ralph A. Bard, Under Secretary of the Navy
William L. Clayton, Assistant Secretary of State

Dr. Karl T. Compton, Chief of the Office of Field Service in the Office of Scientific Research and Development, and president of the Massachusetts Institute of Technology

Dr. Vannevar Bush, Director, Office of Scientific Research and Development, and president of the Carnegie Institution of Washington

Dr. James B. Conant, Chairman of the National Defense Research Committee, and president of Harvard University

This committee "ranged over the whole field of atomic energy, in its political, military, and scientific aspects . . ." as Stimson described it. He said, "The committee's work included the drafting of the statements which were published immediately after the first bombs were dropped, the drafting of a bill for the domestic control of atomic energy, and recommendations looking toward the international control of atomic energy."

But Stimson felt that "the first and greatest problem was the decision on the use of the bomb: Should it be used against the Japanese, and if so, in what manner?"

Before we look into the questions before this committee through the accounts of Compton, Oppenheimer, and Stimson, the military situation needs to be reviewed, for the weapon was not considered in a vacuum.

The Pacific was then the target of massive bombing forces, but strategists differed as to whether bombing alone could ever win in that theater. Most of the high command had already decided that an enormous invasion of Japan would be necessary.

Yet, most of the high command was either unaware or unheeding of a seemingly small ripple in the tides of forces

—the movement of the 509th. The Interim Committee alone, of all such committees at the top of the military pyramid, was in a position to know the facts we may now review.

More than three weeks before this Interim Committee meeting of May 31, the first detachment of the atomic-bomb group had sailed westward with the Navy—for Tinian. This tiny island was in the Marianas, far out in the Pacific, roughly halfway between the Hawaiian Islands and the Philippines.

The 509th Composite Group had received its orders to go to an advance base, there to prepare to carry out its mission whenever it received further orders—and the mysterious "Gimmick."

On May 18 a second advance detachment of the 509th landed by air at Tinian. On May 29, two days before the Interim meeting, a ground echelon unit arrived at Tinian.

Of course, the combat air crews had not yet arrived, and there was a great deal of special preparation still to be done. Everyone was working under emergency conditions, contending with and cursing their way through a maze of red tape and security regulations. Other units of the services, already established on Tinian, did not necessarily snap to attention and move like lightning to accommodate this hybrid Composite Group as it arrived, fresh and green from the States. The 509th was more secretive than most units, and it was not automatically popular or powerful. In motion picture melodrama, this type of all-important, super-secret project usually sweeps everything before it; but in real life such a project often lacks cooperation, simply because people don't know what its purpose is. Tinian was quite busy with things for which it did know the purpose.

Hundreds of thousands of bombs had already been delivered by B-29's flying from the Marianas to Japan, and Tinian at this time was the largest airfield in the world.

Dr. Philip Morrison, a Los Alamos physicist, was sent to join the 509th and described the base in these words:

> I doubt that there is a more complex and wonderful machine in the world than the B-29. And here at Tinian, far from the factories in Seattle and Wichita, were several hundred of these million-dollar craft. Here were collected tens of thousands of specialists trained in the operation and repair of the delicate mechanisms which cram the body of the plane.
>
> In the harbor every day rode tankers, laden with thousands of tons of aviation gasoline. A net of pipe lines supplied the airfields with fuel. The radio dial was busy with signals of every kind.
>
> And all these gigantic preparations had a grand and terrible outcome. At sunset some days the field would be loud with the roar of the motors. Down the great runways would roll the huge planes, seeming to move slowly because of their size, but far outspeeding the occasional racing jeep. One after another, each runway would launch its planes. Once every fifteen seconds another B-29 would become air-borne. For an hour and a half this would continue with precision and order. The sun would go below the sea, and the last planes could still be seen in the distance, with running lights still on.

From such bases, the Asian theater of war was to receive the massive blows that the European theater had already felt.

The whole world—American production men not least of all—had been startled a few years before, when Franklin D. Roosevelt predicted that we would produce 60,000 war planes a year. His estimate later proved to be conservative.

The Fascist nations, at first in Ethiopia and Spain, and most effectively in Hitler's Blitz against the Low Countries, had demonstrated the decisive role of the airplane in total war. The Fascists had shocked the world with fire and destruction, directed against civilian populations. Now they were shocked as they received massive retaliation for their aggressions. American war production centers, which were completely safe from bombing, had reached their peak.

The B-17's—the "Flying Forts"—and then the B-24's and B-29's had appeared, first in dozens and then in hundreds. Against the Nazis, we and the British mounted day and night attacks of 300 and 500 bombers and, ultimately, a thousand planes in a single raid. In the last year of the war, city after city in Europe was pounded in a deluge of destruction such as human beings had never imagined. This earth had never before seen the physical phenomena which now appeared, such as the "fire-storms" in Hamburg.

In the relation of man to nature, the fire-storms were something new. When so many fires are set instantaneously, as in a particular raid on Hamburg, the combined heat of all the fires creates tremendous updrafts; there is a great inrush of air from the outer streets to the center of the blazing city, and this rush of wind is entirely similar to conditions which create natural storms. Strange eddies and cross-currents are set up: there are miniature whirlpools of flame and debris, and the result is a man-made cyclone.

In 1944 and early 1945 the Twentieth Air Force in the

Pacific had set out to bring this same scale of destruction to the home grounds of the Japanese. The air strategists thought Japan offered a vulnerable air target that might prove, once and for all, certain concepts set forth by the classic (but not very ancient) theorists of air power. They believed air power to be supreme: it was not only necessary but would be sufficient to end the war—and any foreseeable future war.

The Pacific had been a secondary theater to the Allies. Raids of a thousand planes each did not seem likely. Furthermore, our bases were considerably farther from the targets than the few hundred miles from England to any part of the Axis heartland. The flight from the Marianas to Honshu, the main Japanese island, for example, was 1400 miles. That did not strain the theoretical capacity of a B-29, but it was not a mere summer's-day glide, either. Almost every inch of the trip was over water.

On the other hand, as compared with Europe, the Japanese cities offered some advantages as targets. It was not quite true that they were paper cities and therefore flimsy. Many of the Japanese buildings, in fact, had been designed with earthquakes in mind, and so were resistant to ordinary man-made blasts. But the Japanese targets were close together; they had many residential sections that would burn like tinder; and, most important of all, they had an incredible population density.

The strategic air planners could virtually mark off an area for destruction and count the casualties beforehand. At a command, hundreds of planes would leave. The pilot-planes would go in first to drop flares and mark off the area; then wave after wave of merciless bombers would follow, dropping the incendiaries and the blast-bombs and utterly destroying an industrial complex or an industrial suburb that had housed tens of thousands of closely packed human beings.

General Curtis LeMay, and others, evolved a new and more terrible bombing pattern. This included night attacks at low level, visual bombing, and fire-bombs in greater numbers. To these tactical changes was added a policy of striking against "areas," not merely against strictly military installations. One reason for this was that much of Japan's war product was fabricated in home workshops.

It may be of interest to look at some samples of "area bombing" as the kind of operation which became familiar, in 1945, to such policy groups as the Interim Committee.

One night a large group of planes from the 314th Wing's 19th and 29th Groups took off from Guam and, soon after, still more planes of the 73rd and 313th Wings left from Saipan and Tinian. It took two and three-quarter hours to get all these planes aloft. There were 334 planes and they carried some 2000 tons of bombs. The pilots were told not to stay in formation but to bomb, at their discretion, whatever was still left for bombing at the time of their arrival. They headed for a rectangle measuring about four by three miles in the capital city of Tokyo.

One ward they would hit—the Asakusa area—had a "built-upness," as Air Corps people called it, of 40 to 50 per cent—which meant that the ratio of roof space to total area was about one to one; whereas an American residential district presents only 10 per cent roof area to a bomber. In the Asakusa ward there were 103,000 persons to the square mile. The Asakusa buildings were mostly of wood-bamboo-plaster construction. Under the fire-bombs, they had no chance.

The first returning radio messages set the pattern for Götterdämmerung, translated from German to Japanese.

"Bombing the target visually. Large fires observed. Flak moderate. Fighter opposition nil."

This district burned, it was said, "like a brush fire in a drought." Late arrivals among the B-29's had to search for targets, there was so little left to blast. They also complained, as many pilots would complain later, of the turbulence caused by the hot-air updrafts or thermals, as they became known. Crews learned to fear thermals as they would fear any other weather front.

Tail-gunners, on the way home from Tokyo that first night, reported they could see the glow of the city for 150 miles. Fifteen square miles of area were destroyed, and about a quarter of a million buildings. Some 85,000 human beings were dead; 40,000 were burned and wounded; and a million persons were homeless.

Less than twenty-nine hours after the last plane had returned from Tokyo, another massive force, this time with 313 B-29's, took off for Nagoya, Japan's third-largest city and hub of her aircraft industry. Nagoya became a symbol of a second-best air power, forced to the ground, being destroyed by a first-class air power. The next morning an American naval ship 150 miles offshore reported that its visibility was cut to one mile because of smoke. That was Nagoya.

Through this spring our air power put the torch to the tinder cities of Japan: Tokyo had a target area of fifty-five square miles and we destroyed fifty-six. Nagoya had sixteen miles of target area and we destroyed twelve, Kobe had only seven square miles of target area, and lost eight. Man-made fire-storms raged through the cities of Japan: Osaka, Yokohama, Kawasaki . . .

Prince Higashuni, Commander-in-Chief of Home Defense Headquarters, admitted defeat to himself:

> The war was lost when the Marianas were taken away from Japan and when we heard the B-29s were coming out . . . we had nothing in Japan that we could use against such a weapon. From the point of view of the Home Defense Command, we felt that the war was lost and said so.

Prince Higashuni was not the only Japanese official who now felt the war was hopeless; but most Japanese military leaders felt differently. Our military men who were meeting the Japanese at "the cutting edge" of their fighting forces did not detect any slackening of their will to resist. The fighting on Iwo Jima had been exceptionally grim. Officially the island was ours in March, but there were many pockets of resistance which held out until weeks later. On larger islands some Japanese were to hold out for years rather than surrender to the hated enemy.

This last year was the period of the kamikazes—the Japanese suicide pilots—who astounded our Navy. These men would come in against all odds and deliberately crash their planes into our ships. In these crashes the Japanese would lose one plane and one pilot, but we would suffer much more damage, sometimes an entire ship.

Such evidence of last-ditch resistance offered us no hope for an easy end to the war. The men at the Chief-of-Staff level, and just below, calculated that very possibly the Japanese will to resist would stay alive to the bitter end—perhaps until our soldiers occupied their territory inch by inch. With this viewpoint, the theorists of Army Infantry considered the Army Air Corps to be visionary in hoping to bring the Japanese to their knees by aerial bombardment alone.

Aerial photographs of post-raid Tokyo and Yokohama at first glance looked like photos of a finely raked garden with craters such as a raindrop makes in fine dust. Whole areas were gone and could not be repaired. New districts would be built, but some districts had essentially vanished. Air Corps men were understandably optimistic about the length of the war and the probable nature of its end.

At the same time, the men who had seen the cornered Japanese fight like caged tigers in their dugouts on Iwo Jima felt quite differently. They thought the war would be cruelly won, and cruelly lost, after Japan was bled white.

It was during this period that Truman said in a letter:

> I know that Japan is a terribly cruel nation in warfare but I can't bring myself to believe that, because they are cruel, we should ourselves act in the same manner. For myself, I certainly regret the necessity of wiping out whole populations because of the "pigheadedness" of the leaders of a nation and, for your information, I am not going to do it unless it becomes absolutely necessary. My object is to save as many American lives as possible but I also have a humane feeling for the women and children in Japan.

Millions of Americans wanted not merely to end the war but to gain emotional satisfaction from the manner of the end: They applauded Admiral Halsey when he said he intended "to ride the Emperor's white horse down the streets of Tokyo."

The men at the very top of the Allied governments were making agonizing decisions in the planning of the war. Some of them deeply felt the responsibility, and also had the opportunity, to think beyond tactics, strategic theory, and emotions of national vengeance. One such man went to see the President.

Joseph C. Grew, at this time an Under Secretary of State, had for many years been our Ambassador to Japan; he had loved the Japanese people and felt that he knew them. He watched with horror the "will to fight" as it rose to new heights on both sides of the Pacific.

By coincidence, Mr. Grew was Acting Secretary of State for some of this period and, with reports of new fire raids upon Tokyo on May 23 and 25, could contain himself no longer. He went to see President Truman and pleaded with him to make a "generous" peace offer to the Japanese. Specifically, he proposed modifications in the Allied doctrine of unconditional surrender. The former Ambassador did not do this merely out of generosity to the almost-vanquished Japanese. Rather, he felt that an earlier approach to the inevitable end would be the most prudent course for the United States and Britain, not to mention the rest of the war-ravaged world. Grew, however, was not the only critic of the policy of unconditional surrender which Truman had inherited from Roosevelt.

One specific point that Grew put to the President was that we permit the Japanese to keep their Emperor. He knew that millions of Americans had seen thousands of war cartoons and war posters showing the three evil countries that had to be utterly beaten. The Axis, moreover, was symbolized by three men who had to be destroyed—Hitler, Mussolini, and Hirohito. These names were household words to millions of people who had bought war bonds, and also made far greater sacrifices, to the end that these evil men should be cut down.

Grew knew the depth of feeling in this country, and he also knew the facts about the military clique that was in control in Japan. Having such deep convictions in this matter, he spoke strongly to Truman.

Grew's idea about the Emperor was in the President's mind, and very much in the mind of Secretary Stimson when the Interim Committee held its momentous meetings; in particular the meetings of May 31 and June 1. This was the first meeting at which high policy-makers considered the bomb program as an important part of national policy.

The Interim Committee met on May 31 and June 1 in the Pentagon.

Of the Interim Committee members, Stimson and Harrison were from the War Department, Bard and Clayton were from the Navy and State Departments, and Byrnes, as we have noted, was a private citizen but, in this group, represented the White House. Bush, Conant, and Karl Compton were scientists, and all three of them were at that moment on leave from their private posts and were administering government scientific agencies.

However, since these three scientists were not involved in day-to-day work in laboratories, it was found appropriate to appoint a further advisory panel of scientists whose duty would be to furnish technical information. This advisory panel consisted of Arthur Compton (Karl Compton's brother), Enrico Fermi, Ernest O. Lawrence, and J. Robert Oppenheimer. These four men had been scientists and administrators on the Manhattan Project. All, except Fermi, had more than the usual interest a scientist takes in ethical and political questions arising from his work. All except Oppenheimer had won the Nobel Prize for exceptional work in physics.

This Interim Committee had many technical questions: How certain was it that the bomb would work? Could it be dropped from an airplane? What would happen if it did not explode?

The men of the advisory panel were invited to attend the first day of the Committee meeting, and it quickly became apparent that these scientists would not merely answer and raise technical questions, but would be welcome to participate fully in all discussions. They could and did raise questions which the others might or might not have considered:

Was this merely a superbomb? Should Japan be warned that a new kind of destruction had been brought into the world? Should the bomb be dropped, as a demonstration, on uninhabited territory? Could the atomic development be kept a secret if the bomb were not used at all? Could other countries make such bombs; and if so, how soon?

The meeting of May 31 was also attended by General Leslie R. Groves, and by General George C. Marshall, Chief of Staff of the Army. These two represented the military, and it may be noted that they were the only men in uniform. The generals were far outnumbered, though definitely not outranked, by the scientists.

It was seven weeks since Truman had become President, and it would be seven weeks more before the bomb could actually be tested, but there was little doubt at this meeting that the experiment would work.

As Dr. Compton recalls it, in his book *Atomic Quest,* the meeting began with an electric and eloquent statement by Secretary Stimson: "Gentlemen, it is our responsibility to recommend action that may turn the course of civilization. In our hands we expect soon to have a weapon of wholly unprecedented destructive power."

Compton had never met Stimson before, and was impressed then and later with the vigor of a man his age. "Stimson had a spirit so strong it kept him alive and alert," Compton has said.

Stimson then continued: "Today's prime fact is war. Our great task is to bring this war to a prompt and successful conclusion. We may assume that our new weapon puts in our hands overwhelming power. It is our obligation to use this power with the best wisdom we can command."

Stimson also emphasized the point he had already emphasized to the President: "To us now the matter of first importance is how our use of this new weapon will appear in the long view of history."

First, the Committee was given a summary of the technical questions about the bomb. What could the bomb do, and how could it be delivered? How many such bombs could we make, and at what rate?

As already indicated in Chapter 5, the problems of timing and implosion of parts of fissionable material toward one another are matters of great intricacy and delicacy. In a word, it was not easy to make an atomic bomb that would explode. The Army was planning a test to be held approximately seven weeks from the time of the Interim meeting. It was expected that the bomb would work; if it did, it would be an explosion indeed. The supply of bombs thereafter would be extremely limited. Since they were made virtually by hand, perhaps one or two other bombs would be ready soon after the test. Thereafter, the production facilities might deliver one bomb every few weeks.

The first combat models of the bomb could be exploded by the proximity fuse, another secret development which contributed greatly to the Allied victory in the closing months of the war. A device very much like a radar transmitter, the proximity fuse was attached to a bomb or shell and sent out a signal to the target, and through a radar receiver "heard" the signal bounce back. When the echo came back within a specified definite time interval, the device triggered the bomb. Thus, a bomb with such a device attached could be dropped, and when its control gave the signal for the bomb to detonate, it would automatically go off.

As the scientists explained, it was believed that the major military use of the bomb would be the blast-effect of its explosion. The principal effect would be not fire or radiation, but simply and literally a *crushing* effect—a giant block-buster. To cause the maximum damage, the bomb was to be set off some distance above the ground, for its blast was expected to carry some distance. Army and Air Force planners, led by General Groves, had long before this realized that this superbomb could do blast damage at a half-mile or a mile away—or even further.

This ability to cause damage by one big blast, in the

opinion of Oppenheimer and other technical advisers, pointed toward using the bomb on a concentration of troops or war plants, which, in Compton's words, could be "put out of commission" by the explosion.

How many people would be killed by such a bomb dropped on a city?

Speaking as a technician, Dr. Oppenheimer answered that 20,000 people would probably be killed. He, and everyone else, assumed that Japanese cities usually had some system of air-raid warning before a raid, and thus the estimate and subsequent decisions were based on the erroneous belief that most people would have found some kind of shelter before such a bomb exploded.

Would the atomic bomb go off?

The military and scientific leaders were certain it would. Compton has said he was certain of it some months before this meeting. He places his certainty back as far as December, 1944, which agrees with the official word of General Groves.

How secret could the bomb be kept if it were not used?

General Marshall said that he would be against the use of the new weapon, other things being equal, if it were felt we could continue to keep its existence secret after the war. Use of the bomb would show that we had it, giving other countries an incentive to build bombs, too. If it could be kept quite secret, it would put us in a stronger military position, relative to countries without it, for some years ahead. In his opinion, the weapon was not absolutely needed; it would be costly but possible to win without it.

A discussion of secrecy followed this statement by the Chief of Staff. The scientists present were unanimous: the general outlines of the new atomic knowledge were sure to become known at the end of the war. Compton felt that this did not fully answer General Marshall's objections, for even with general knowledge available, the details of the bomb might still be kept secret for some time, within the U.S. and Britain. And it could certainly be argued that if the bomb were not exploded, other nations would not have the compelling incentive to develop it.

Later, in talking to General Marshall, Dr. Compton learned that the Chief of Staff had raised the secrecy question as one that ought to be answered, but that he himself had gone to the meeting with the conclusion that the bomb ought to be used. Marshall did not, however, want to present this view at the outset and thus prejudice the civilian group which had been asked to consider policy. Marshall told Compton that he could not believe that Japan could be forced to surrender solely as a result of air and naval bombardment, and therefore one had to consider either a long war—or some special means of ending it.

Compton has written, "Throughout the morning's discussions it seemed to be a foregone conclusion that the bomb would be used. It was only in regard to the details of strategy and tactics that differing views were expressed."

But, at luncheon, Compton brought into the open the question that would never be completely answered.

Did the first A-bomb have to be aimed to kill? Could not the first one be dropped as a nonmilitary demonstration?

Or could the bomb be announced—then exploded—with

the purpose of asking Japan to surrender before any more of them were dropped—and upon human beings?

At luncheon Compton was seated next to Stimson. "In the course of conversation I asked the Secretary whether it might not be possible to arrange a nonmilitary demonstration . . . in such a manner . . . the Japanese . . . would see the uselessness of continuing the war."

Compton's remark made a deep impression upon Stimson, who had been considering such an idea himself. He asked the general conversation to stop, and put the question to the entire table. Various suggestions were discussed and deemed unlikely to work. One problem, of course, was that each side in the war was quite willing to believe the other was bluffing or pulling some trick.

We would have to be quite careful to prove to the Japanese that we possessed what we said we possessed. Therefore, we should most likely have to explode one on Japanese territory. We could not very well announce in advance when and where we would do it, since no one considered Japan's air defenses to be absolutely powerless. No one, except perhaps air-power enthusiasts, was willing to say flatly that we could pick a date and be absolutely sure that on that date a bomb could, without fail, be delivered to such and such an uninhabited mountaintop or desert plain on one of Japan's main islands.

The intricate bomb was still in the developmental stage. Saying that one could make atomic bombs was quite different from saying that one could make a success of every one of them, especially under combat conditions. If one advertised a demonstration and then produced a dud, the results for peace would be worse than if one had not tried at all.

Of this possibility, Mr. Byrnes said:

> We feared that, if the Japanese were told that the bomb would be used on a given locality, they might bring our boys who were prisoners of war to that area. Also, the experts had warned us that the static test which was to take place in New Mexico, even if successful, could not be conclusive proof that a bomb would explode when dropped from an airplane. If we were to warn the Japanese of the new highly destructive weapon in the hope of impressing them and if the bomb then failed to explode, certainly we would have given aid and comfort to the Japanese militarist. Thereafter, the Japanese people probably would not be impressed by any statement we might make in the hope of inducing them to surrender.

It also appeared that there would be all-too-long intervals between the completion of each bomb.

Would a test over neutral territory be the answer? Compton wrote, "It was hard to believe that Japan's determined and fanatical military men would be impressed."

If an open test were made and failed to bring surrender, then we would have lost forever the chance to deliver the shock surprise which is sometimes all-important in war. ". . . the possibility of a demonstration that would not destroy human lives was attractive," said Compton, but "no one could suggest a way in which it would be made so convincing that it would be likely to stop the war."

After luncheon the Interim Committee asked the scientists to wait while the Committee itself met in private session, after which the scientists were called in again.

Stimson asked them "to prepare a report as to whether we could devise any kind of demonstration that would seem likely to bring the war to an end without using the bomb against a live target."

Oppenheimer invited Lawrence, Fermi, and Compton to spend a long weekend at Los Alamos ten days later, during which they could put their heads together.

In his testimony at his security hearing in 1954, Dr. Oppenheimer has said of this group and its meeting at the bomb-making center:

> We didn't know beans about the military situation in Japan. We didn't know whether they could be caused to surrender by other means or whether the invasion was really inevitable. But in back of our minds was the notion that the invasion was inevitable because we had been told that . . .
>
> We said that we didn't think that being scientists especially qualified us as to how to answer this question of how the bombs should be used or not; opinion was divided among us as it would be among other people if they knew about it. We thought the two overriding considerations were the saving of lives in the war and the effects of our actions on our strength and the stability of the postwar world.

The scientists and the Interim Committee as a whole voted against *demonstration,* and for *military use* of the bomb.

We shall later take a closer look at this verdict, but we must also note other advice reaching the Pentagon at this same period.

The Scientific Panel's report was given to the Interim Committee on June 16, but before that time Stimson's office was to hear from other scientists, men who felt quite strongly about *the dangers the bomb would bring to America.* To these counsels Stimson listened with sharp ear and heavy heart. He was a man who could write:

"I see too many stern and heart-rending decisions to pretend that war is anything else than what it is. The face of war is the face of death."

Stimson was not to accept the Interim Committee's conclusions and consider that the decision was final. A Secretary of War is not usually asked to consider using a bomb *as a message,* instead of using it as a bomb—but this was an unusual Secretary.

In the next chapter we shall take a closer look at Stimson and, following that, go over some of the things that the Interim Committee and the other scientists wanted him—and the President—to understand.

7.

"The Old Eagle"

HENRY L. STIMSON had had an extraordinary career, one of the most striking things about it being that it covered four decades of the violent twentieth century. He began this career in the gaslit receptions of the William Howard Taft era, and lived to see the gas chambers of Buchenwald and Dachau.

The new President had been residing in the White House for less than thirty-five days, but this old man had been going in and out of the White House gates for nearly thirty-five years. Few men in American history have endured so long and remained so close to the thrones of power. At seventy-seven, though slightly stooped, Stimson did not look frail or feeble and he was a hard-working Secretary. His hair was white but his piercing eyes and his voice were steady; his orderly mind and judicial manner tended to give him a commanding position in any council. He might break up a Cabinet meeting with a joke if he found himself bored by too steady a diet of seriousness, but most of the time he had the dignity of an eagle.

One of Stimson's cardinal principles was to trust other men. He himself said that the best way to ensure that a man was worthy of trust was to trust him. Stimson trusted lesser men as much as great men trusted him. His philosophy would support the description, "a man with a great deal of faith," but he certainly did not wear his beliefs where an outsider could see them. His memoirs do not mention religion or prayer, and it does not appear that Stimson's belief in the human enterprise was related to convictions of a superhuman power.

Superficially, one might have assumed that this gentlemanly conservative drew his serenity from a background of pattern and comfort, but it is not quite true that he had had all the advantages.

His mother died in 1876, when he was nine years old, and young Henry saw some lonely and hard times. He and his sister were sent to live with grandparents. Later he was sent to Phillips Academy, at Andover, and at the time he was the youngest boy there. He attended Yale and the Harvard Law School, and ever afterward he would speak well, but quite differently, of both schools. Perhaps this is indicative of the attitude he would so often take in later life: he seemed to be quite loyal to any organization to which he belonged. Indeed, he was the very standard by which loyalty could be measured.

Still, Stimson could usually understand the virtues or viewpoint of the other camp. He possessed this attitude early, as a young lawyer in the seething politics of New York City. Stimson was later considered a lifelong Republican, but when Grover Cleveland raised the tariff issue in 1892, Stimson felt that the man was right and he voted Democratic. Later, as Stimson put it, Tammany Hall "was of such a character as to make the path of a young Democrat difficult to follow."

In 1894 he enrolled and worked in the campaign as a Republican. That year he met and began a friendship with Theodore Roosevelt that was to last until the latter died in 1919. Roosevelt made him United States attorney for the Southern District of New York. It was thus that Stimson "crossed the river" into public life, and from then on he felt that public service was a way in which "I could get a good deal closer to the problems of life than I ever did before."

Stimson was pushed into the political arena by Theodore Roosevelt at a time when Charles Evans Hughes, then Governor of New York, was appointed to the Supreme Court. Roosevelt insisted that he run for governor. Stimson was under no illusion that he could win an election at the time, but the Roosevelt wing of the party wanted to be sure that a man of their kind carried the standard in the race.

Stimson did not have any natural affinity for the hurly-burly of campaigning and felt no real identification with crowds of voters. His legal assistant in the district attorney's office, a young man named Felix Frankfurter, once heard Roosevelt trying to loosen up Stimson's style of speaking. "Darn it, Harry," Frankfurter heard him tell Stimson, "a campaign speech is a poster, not an etching!"

Stimson was defeated by an ample margin, and later was to say that "nothing about the campaign of 1910 in New York was as important to Stimson as the simple fact that he did not win." Winning the governorship of New York, of course, would have launched him as a popular political figure on the national stage. Hughes and Theodore Roosevelt and later FDR, Al Smith, and Thomas E. Dewey were to be New York governors and then presidential candidates.

When President Taft, in the middle of his term, was looking for a Secretary of War, he wanted a man who commanded respect in both Republican camps. (Party members were already becoming known as "Taft men" or "Roosevelt men.") Taft asked Stimson and the latter, to be very fair, consulted Roosevelt before accepting the post. The course was cleared and Stimson, at the comparatively young age of forty-three, became a Secretary of War who presided over a peaceful and sleepy Army composed of 4388 officers and 70,230 enlisted men.

Stimson's command at that time did not include as many persons as would work on a single project in Stimson's later career, when 100,000 persons worked to produce the bomb, S-1.

In that long-past spring of 1911 Americans, having recovered from the excitement of the Spanish-American War, were not thinking of any future war. They were more concerned about trusts and about "malefactors of great wealth," as Theodore Roosevelt decribed them. Americans were beginning to know the automobile, and the Wright brothers had become famous after their successful flight in 1908. But a typical American had no idea, as he talked about David Warfield in *The Music Master* and Maude Adams in *Peter Pan,* that the world of 1914 and 1941 would be so different from that of 1911. Harry Truman was twenty-six years old, and had not yet become even a Captain of Artillery.

However, Albert Einstein had already put the special theory of relativity behind him and was on his way to his general theory of relativity. He had already established that there is a definite mass equivalent of energy; the now-famous formula, $E = mc^2$, was born in 1905.

In Russia at this time there was already a special following around the personality of Joseph Dzhugashvili, then known as "Comrade Koba" and later to be known as "the man of steel"—Stalin. The accounts of his life in 1911 differ markedly, depending on whether you are reading an official history, such as Laurenti Beria's, or an unofficial one, such as Leon Trotsky's.

This much is certain: "Comrade Koba" was coming out of exile in 1911 and was seeking a place on the Central Committee—the ruling committee of a Party which, in that year, was only an underground movement against the Czar. Either the exile of "Koba" had ended and he went home peacefully, as Trotsky describes it; or he made another of his famous and dashing escapes, described by Soviet encyclopedists. We do know that "Comrade Koba" was already close to Lenin and was the foe of Trotsky. And he was on his way to becoming the modern Czar of All the Russias—Premier Josef Stalin.

8.

"The Under Side of the Bomb"

DURING THE YEARS OF darkness, while the shape of the coming world was a secret to all men, many scientists lay awake at night pondering their fears—of war, of peace, and of new wars. Never before had scientists played such a part in history. Some felt personally responsible.

The atomic-bomb project started when a few scientists prevailed upon Albert Einstein to write President Roosevelt the now-famous letter suggesting that uranium could be used to make "an extremely powerful bomb." The men who called on Einstein that July of 1939 were Edward Teller, Eugene Wigner, and Leo Szilard.

Dr. Szilard had been a partner of Fermi in the decisive experiments which established sustained nuclear fission. He personally tapped out the historic letter for Einstein to sign.

Fermi and Szilard were among the key scientists who foresaw that the atomic age was inevitable in our generation. The world would change because they had found "spontaneous emission of neutrons in fission." Fermi, of course, had thoughts about what a fission-chain reaction might mean to mankind, but he only permitted himself to express his social ideas obliquely or under a cloak of irony. "If only it could cure the common cold," was one of his comments. Fermi took little outward interest in politics and usually dismissed the subject by saying, "The business of scientists is science." After the war he did not ordinarily join his colleagues in signing statements, joining groups, or appearing on letterheads.

Szilard, however, was constantly thinking of the social and political results of science and inventions. Taking the most current results of the fission experiments to Einstein in 1939, and starting the interest of the government in uranium, was itself a political act. Thus, Szilard sat at the typewriter to produce the letter which some say "ended the childhood of man."

In that fall of 1939 Szilard successfully urged nuclear physicists to keep important findings secret and no longer publish their results in the usual scientific journals. Nearly everyone in science agreed with him, and thereby he led physicists into an underground of secrecy from which they have not emerged to this day. It was later to be said of Leo Szilard that he had been instrumental in developing two terrible threats to man's survival—the atomic bomb and atomic scientific secrecy. But his purpose was the protection of freedom.

In 1939 Szilard saw secrecy and the bomb as threats to Hitler. In 1945 he saw secrecy and the bomb as threats to the human race.

In March of 1945 Szilard prepared a long memorandum, which he hoped to send or bring to the attention of President Roosevelt. He sent the letter, but never saw the President. On May 28, just before the Interim Committee first met,

Szilard was able to reach James Byrnes in a personal interview at Spartanburg, South Carolina. Byrnes was somewhat impressed at the time, but later he heard from other physicists who disagreed with Szilard. Byrnes then made the remark, "In this age it appears every man must have his own physicist."

We shall come back to Szilard and his memo, but let us first look at another project in which Szilard was involved. By early 1945 many scientists on the Manhattan Project were not only searching their own consciences but also discussing among themselves their fears about the bomb and the future. This was especially the case within the ranks of the "informed" scientists working under the code name Metallurgical Laboratory at the University of Chicago.

Here was a galaxy of scientific talent to be matched only by Los Alamos at the same, or slightly later, time. Arthur Compton, the chief of the Chicago group, had a role akin to the director of the Metropolitan Opera: he had to deal with genius and talent on every hand—scientists such as Fermi, Szilard, Urey, and Samuel K. Allison, T. R. Hogness, Herbert L. Anderson, Eugene Rabinowitch, Cecil Smith, and James Franck. Many of these men had seen a good deal of the world. They not only asked questions of nature, they asked questions about man and society. Night after night they talked of how and whether man could survive the tomorrow they foresaw.

Franck, a refugee like many of the others, was a Nobel-Prize-winning chemist of the first rank. But his place in history may rest upon the prophetic letter—later referred to as the Franck Report—that he, Eugene Rabinowitch, and Leo Szilard wrote to Henry L. Stimson. The exact time of its arrival is not too clear, but Dr. Compton (in a letter to the author) is certain that it was before the first official meeting of the Interim Committee. Other accounts place it "later than" June 11. In any case, Franck's letter arrived at Stimson's office in June of 1945, and was discussed there about the same time the Interim Committee was holding its crucial meetings.

In retrospect, all concerned could regret that Stimson and Franck were never brought together. James Franck might ordinarily be identified as a German, a Jew, a chemist, a Nobel Laureate. He had also been an officer in Kaiser Wilhelm's army. Perhaps, for this story, he might best be identified as a European from that Europe which used to be.

Long before this time—at the outbreak of World War I—Franck was doing work which added to man's understanding of atomic structure. Then the war drew him into the army, and he earned the rank of captain. This was considered an exceptional distinction for a person not of the German military caste system, either by heredity or by long training.

After the war Franck returned to his laboratory at the University of Göttingen, and found it completely bare of equipment. From his own pocket he supplied money for instruments to build up the laboratory again. His genius, and the men he attracted to Göttingen, added much to the university's fame in the history of nuclear physics, which is to say, in the history of the world. Many bright young men from America went there to study—among them were Karl T. Compton and J. Robert Oppenheimer.

In 1926 Franck won the Nobel Prize. The night of the announcement, University students held an impromptu torchlight procession through the ancient streets of Göttingen. But, in the years to follow, as Hitlerism progressed, the conditions for free scientists became worse and worse, and Franck was moved to protest through public statements. Soon after, it became apparent that Germany would become unsafe for him, in spite of his scientific achievements and brilliant war record.

Franck made plans to flee, and he and his colleague Max von Laue smuggled their gold Nobel medals to a scientist-friend in Denmark, to keep for them. They did not want such identifying valuables with them in their flight. Franck came to the United States, going first to the Massachusetts Institute of Technology and eventually to the University of Chicago.

The war spread, and as the Nazis approached Denmark, the scientist who had custody of Franck's and Von Laue's medals learned that the occupation troops were approaching his laboratory. It has been said that since the man was a genius he could not do anything so simple as to bury the medals in the garden; the janitor might have thought of that. Instead, this scientist dissolved the medals in acid and suspended the gold in solution.

Word that the medals were "safe" eventually reached Franck. Being in an old brown laboratory bottle, which the Nazis completely overlooked, the gold could probably be recovered someday—if Franck cared that much for it. Meanwhile the Nobel stamp of approval was not needed for Franck to be honored by American scientists. So Franck had the honor and the gold was safe. He had lost temporarily only a certain amount of bas-relief sculpture. After the war Franck's dissolved medal, in its bottle, was sent to the Nobel

Institute and the gold was again pressed into a medal. Franck is the only man who ever received his Nobel medal twice: the one before the Nazis, and the same one after. But no one was able by any aid of art or science to mold again the Europe that was. No one can give back to Professor Franck his old University of Göttingen and his free world of scholars. By the spring of 1945, the professor had twicc seen the treasures of man's spirit destroyed by war.

Professor Franck was not yet even a naturalized citizen at the time Arthur Compton was looking for someone to head a chemistry project within the atomic enterprise. As James Bryant Conant and Arthur Compton talked about the talents required, Conant finally asked, "If you had your pick of anyone in the country, whom would you choose?" Compton named Franck. But, technically, Franck was an enemy alien and could not be hired by the Army.

Yet, when the subject came up, five of the six members of the relevant committee vouched for Franck personally. In those days security clearance procedure was such that K. D. Nichols, the Army Colonel in charge, was able to say, "This is a much more reliable judgment than any official review could afford . . ." (Nichols had changed his mind about official reviews by the time he wrote Oppenheimer, in 1953, suspending Oppenheimer's clearance, provoking the most arduous official review in the history of the Security System.)

Franck was quite pleased to join the project. He was later to become an American citizen, and to enjoy the rare distinction of being elected to the National Academy of Sciences by acclamation.

Within the atomic project, he proved to have exceptional

dexterity at managing things so as to help independent and brilliant minds work together.

In the winter season of 1944-45, as the scientists more and more often turned to nonscientific questions raised by the bomb, Franck was a natural leader in the discussions. Eventually a semi-official committee was formed, a Committee on Social and Political Implications, and Franck was named Chairman.

The names of the members of this group have been officially held secret to this day, but some are known. Among them were D. Hughes, Joyce Stearns, Glenn Seaborg, and J. J. Nickson, and two of the most active members were Leo Szilard and Eugene Rabinowitch. The latter was a Russian-born chemist who possessed the unusual combination of first-class scientific ability and first-class literary skill.

Rabinowitch worked at the actual writing of the 1945 document addressed to Stimson, in the same way that Leo Szilard had done six years before, when he, Teller, Wigner, and Einstein communicated with President Roosevelt.

That spring Franck and Rabinowitch and the others worked, with a great sense of responsibility, drafting and redrafting various sections of their statement; Leo Szilard made important additions. They worked mainly at Chicago, and the document, since it dealt with secret matters, had to be locked up like any other secret material. Their main concern was that the leaders of the country should think carefully before using this energy as a weapon, and in fact should perhaps not use it at all.

Franck's group did not know what to call their document, and it finally became known as the Franck Report. Despite the precedent of writing to the White House, set by

Einstein in 1939, they more modestly addressed their remarks to the Secretary of War.

Why did these men, men of cold logic and objective method, work at writing such an unofficial letter to high authorities—who might not be interested?

We may judge they wrote it because they were afraid—afraid that all the treasures of man—and man himself—might be destroyed in the next war.

In 1939 Szilard and his colleagues were thinking of the atom in World War II.

In 1945 they were having nightmares of the atom in World War III.

The preamble to the Franck Report to the Secretary of War began with the expression of fear that atomic bombs someday might fall upon the free world, and that scientists did not foresee adequate defenses against such atomic weapons:

"All of us," they wrote, meaning the scientists working in secret, "familiar with the present state of nucleonics, live with the vision before our eyes of sudden destruction visited on our own country, of a Pearl Harbor disaster repeated in thousand-fold magnification in every one of our major cities."

They said that, in the past, science had often been able to provide new protection against new methods of aggression, but that this could not be expected for the super-destructive weapons of the future. Thus, they said, protection for the human race had to come "from the political organization of the world."

On secrecy, they concluded that there was no chance of keeping the basic development secret. Nor did they think we could keep so many secrets as to remain far ahead of other countries, and thereby be so superior that others would not attack. They completely rejected the arguments of national strength-through-secrecy.

On Russia, they said, "The experience of Russian scientists in nuclear research is entirely sufficient to enable them to retrace our steps within a few years, even if we should make every attempt to conceal them."

On the balance of power, they saw little hope in having any major power assume that its basic industrial strength could protect it in the new age. The report said that these weapons would put a premium upon surprise attack. Enemy bombs could even be hidden in major cities and touched off by remote control. They foresaw something that they had begun to call "suitcase warfare."

The Report pointed out that we were a country with concentrated population, but that we might be opposing some country "whose industry and population are dispersed over a large territory." This latter point they repeated in the hope that it would not be missed.

On the atomic armament race, they gave a warning:

> If no efficient international agreement is achieved, the race for nuclear armaments will be on in earnest not later than the morning after our first demonstration of the existence of nuclear weapons.
>
> After this, it might take other nations three or four years to overcome our head start, and eight or ten years to draw even with us if we continue to do intensive work in this field.

On the prospects of world agreement, the scientists were not optimistic, further adding that as scientists they did "not presume to speak authoritatively on problems of national and international policy." But, they thought, prospects of nuclear warfare and the alternatives to world law would "be as abhorrent to other nations as to the United States."

They came to a main conclusion that "only lack of mutual trust, and not lack of desire for agreement, can stand in the path of an efficient agreement for the prevention of nuclear warfare." They thought that "the achievement of such an agreement will thus essentially depend on the integrity of intentions and readiness to sacrifice the necessary fraction of one's own sovereignty, by all the parties to the agreement."

With this background introduction, the men, led by Franck, turned to the specific question of various ways to use the bomb then being prepared.

On use of the bomb, they thought that Allied statesmen should be looking forward to a world that would have established control over atomic bombs, and that "a demonstration of the new weapon might best be made, before the eyes of representatives of all the United Nations, on a desert or barren island." They thought that:

> . . . the best possible atmosphere for the achievement of an international agreement could be achieved if America could say to the world, "You see what sort of weapon we had but did not use. We are ready to renounce its use in the future if other nations join us in this renunciation and agree to the establishment of an efficient international control."

The Franck Report authors suggested that, after a demonstration, the bomb might be used against Japan, "with the sanction of the United Nations and public opinion at home." They assumed that first Japan might be given an ultimatum to surrender or to evacuate certain regions. "This may sound fantastic," they argued, "but in nuclear weapons we have something entirely new in order of magnitude of destructive power, and if we want to capitalize fully on the advantage their possession gives us, we must use new and imaginative methods."

On using the bomb without warning, the Franck group thought that:

> . . . the question of the use of the very first available bombs . . . should be weighed very carefully, not only by military authorities, but by the highest political leadership of this country. Russia, and even allied countries which bear less mistrust of our ways and intentions, as well as neutral countries, may be deeply shocked by this step. It may be very difficult to persuade the world that a nation which was capable of secretly preparing and suddenly releasing a new weapon, as indiscriminate as the rocket bomb and a thousand times more destructive, is to be trusted in its proclaimed desire of having such weapons abolished by international agreement. . . . It is not at all certain that American public opinion, if it could be enlightened as to the effect of atomic explosives, would approve of our own country being the first to introduce such an indiscriminate method of wholesale destruction of civilian life.

In conclusion, the scientists said that an atomic arms race would place the United States at a disadvantage, because of her concentrated population. Thus, they said, "We believe that these considerations make the use of nuclear bombs for an early unannounced attack against Japan inadvisable." They thought that if one assumed that world control of atomic weapons could not be achieved, then the longer one put off the use of atomic bombs, the better. For, the moment they were used the human race would enter upon history's most dangerous arms race. Eventually our enemies would have them. That day could be postponed by not using the bombs ourselves.

The Franck Report not only looked through the sights of this proposed weapon, it was remarkable because it turned the weapon around and looked into its muzzle. Or, to bring the figure of speech more up-to-date, these men did not merely look down upon the bomb, as a bombardier does when the bomb is falling away—they could view the under side of the bomb.

Not until Sputnik would many Americans realize how different such weapons might look from the under side.

Now the timetable of events should be recalled:

On June 1 the Interim Committee "recommended that the bomb should be used against Japan, without specific warning, as soon as possible, and against such a target as to make clear its devastating strength." Ralph Bard, representing the Navy on this Committee, thought it over further and later sent a note dissenting from the recommendation that it be used without warning. Otherwise, it remained unanimous. The Scientific Advisory Panel had not yet reported.

Perhaps it was earlier, but by June 11 the Franck Report had been delivered to Secretary Stimson's office. On this same day the combat air crews of the 509th were flying over the Pacific, toward their destination, Tinian. They did not, of course, carry the bombs—none had yet been made.

On June 16 the Scientific Advisory Panel, which had met informally with Oppenheimer at Los Alamos, reported back to the Interim Committee. The hearts of Fermi, Lawrence, Oppenheimer, and Compton were heavy as they reported, in a sentence which Stimson would underline and never forget, *"We can propose no technical demonstration likely to bring an end to the war; we see no acceptable alternative to direct military use."*

The reasoning behind these recommendations has been set out by Stimson, Compton, and others:

First of all, it should be noted that the Interim Committee was appointed not to make a decision but to give advice. As Stimson put it, "The committee's function was, of course, entirely advisory. The ultimate responsibility for the recommendation to the President rested upon me, and I have no desire to veil it. The conclusions of the committe were similar to my own, although I reached mine independently."

The Interim Committee had made up their minds as of June 1, but they still did not want to close the door to the possibility of some other alternative than ordinary military use. If they had actually been the body that had to make the decision, they would have been required to do so on June 1 or some other date. But since they were advisory, they could give their advice and then go further and ask the scientists attached to the Committee to keep working on the examination of alternative courses. So they recommended one course and yet asked the scientists to work on another and, furthermore, to report upon the judgment of the scientific community. The scientists' opinions would also be merely advisory to the War Secretary, who was to advise the President.

Neither the Interim Committee nor the Scientific Panel,

apparently, had before it the text of the Franck Report; but Compton had gone over it with Franck. The Scientific Panel was familiar with the reasoning of colleagues opposed to initial military use of the bomb.

The Scientific Panel's summation, as given by Stimson and verified by members of the Panel, went like this:

> The opinions of our scientific colleagues on the initial use of these weapons are not unanimous; they range from the proposal of a purely technical demonstration to that of the military application best designed to induce surrender. Those who advocate a purely technical demonstration would wish to outlaw the use of atomic weapons, and have feared that if we use the weapons now our position in future negotiations will be prejudiced. Others emphasize the opportunity of saving American lives by immediate military use, and believe that such use will improve the international prospects, in that they are more concerned with the prevention of war than with the elimination of this special weapon. We find ourselves closer to these latter views:
>
> *We can propose no technical demonstration likely to bring an end to the war; we see no acceptable alternative to direct military use.*

The italics are those of Mr. Stimson.

The idea of a demonstration did not appeal to any of the scientists on this panel. As Oppenheimer later said, "We did say that we did not think exploding one of these things as a firecracker over a desert was likely to be very impressive. This was before we had actually done that."

We will examine Stimson's reasoning in more detail later on, but to him, it did not appear certain that a demonstration could have significant effect. His military strategists—General Marshall in particular—were emphatic in their opinion that the surprise and the shock value of military use could be decisive to the war.

The kind of thinking represented in the Franck Report was neither strange nor new to Stimson. However, he assumed—and this involved then and involves now a value judgment—that these alternate lines of reasoning had received the fullest consideration by the Scientific Panel, after preliminary consultation with the Interim group.

As Compton describes it, the issues "had long been foreseen by General Groves," and:

> Franck's statement made two major points . . . the killing of thousands of people . . . was morally reprehensible . . . [and] would develop an attitude of fear, suspicion, and hate toward the United States . . . the second point was that the United States might eventually wish to outlaw the use of atomic weapons by international agreement . . . but if our nation had already used atomic bombs, it would be in a weak position to recommend their prohibition. . . .

According to Compton, Franck's "study was in progress when word reached them that President Truman was consulting with the Secretary of War. . . . They . . . accordingly hastened to draft their conclusions."

Franck himself took the Report to Washington, and Compton tried to bring him and the Secretary together. Stimson was out of the city, but George Harrison, Acting Chairman of the Interim Committee and a special consultant to Stimson, told Compton he would personally see that the Secretary considered the Franck Report.

Compton did not turn over the document until he had added a covering note calling attention to what he considered deficiencies. There is no mention by Stimson in his memoirs of receiving this specific document, nor of Franck's and Compton's views. However, Compton's comment to Stimson was that the report "called attention to difficulties . . . did not mention the probable net saving of many lives, nor that if the bomb were not used in the present war the world would have no adequate warning as to what was to be expected if war should break out again."

This unofficial letter from Franck, with the Compton note, and the firm official recommendation of the Scientific Panel were not to be the last word heard from the scientists on this subject.

These two reports in the middle of June sent the decision upstairs. Before we move on to what the Joint Chiefs of Staff and the White House were considering, we will look at some of the activity going on in the underworld of espionage.

9.

"I Come from Julius"

IN 1945 THERE WERE several Russian espionage groups operating in the United States and Canada, and a man named Harry Gold was one of four scientist-agents concerned with the A-bomb project. Through his connections with Fuchs and Greenglass, Gold was the agent who was busiest during the period of our story, as we shall soon see.

A year before this period, according to testimony at his trial, Julius Rosenberg had received and transmitted atomic information. In fact, Rosenberg reputedly knew enough about Los Alamos, the bomb-making center, to be able to pass on information to his sister Ruth Greenglass. She was the one who first informed her husband, David, of what was going on in New Mexico, since, under security restrictions, a mere machinist like Greenglass was given little information. Greenglass, although he was working at Los Alamos, learned of the atomic bomb from the outside.

Rosenberg has mistakenly been considered the most important of "the atomic spies"; whereas actually he was never employed on any atomic project and his closest brush with nuclear secrets was in arranging contacts for his brother-in-law, Greenglass. And even though the latter was at a key installation, many respected scientists, such as Harold C. Urey, have said that Greenglass simply did not have the technical background to transmit highly detailed or comprehensive information.

There were others, however, who did have the background. The man who combined unusual intelligence, advanced education, and complete access to top-secret information was the ideal scientist-agent, Klaus Fuchs. He was a theoretical physicist, working on the most complex and most secret scientific problems of "manhattan." Even at the time of our story, he was in on the considerations of J. Robert Oppenheimer, Hans Bethe, and Edward Teller on hydrogen-fusion reactions, which later led to the H-bomb.

There were two other scientifically trained minds in the other Soviet underground groups:

Two years before, Alan Nunn May had arrived on the Canadian end of the atomic project, in Montreal. He was to be the first spy to come to public attention, after his Russian contact, Igor Gouzenko, defected from the Russian Embassy in Canada.

Bruno Pontecorvo, an excellent scientist and a former colleague of Enrico Fermi, also came to Canada in 1943. He was first at McGill University in Montreal, but then was transferred to the Canadian atomic installation at Chalk River. In 1944 Pontecorvo had visited the secret atomic laboratory of the Manhattan Project in Chicago, the "Metallurgical Laboratory." Pontecorvo later defected to Russia, after disappearing with his wife and family in Finland, in October of 1950. He and May knew each other in Montreal, and he and Fuchs were later acquainted at Harwell, England. But the officials who have investigated these cases believe that probably each of the three did not know that the other two were also agents. The Russian espionage machinery apparently kept these people in quite separate compartments.

Like so many others whom we will meet as this history unfolds, Harry Gold was in the dark as to the ultimate goal of his missions. He neither met nor knew of the existence of Rosenberg during his spy career. "I come from Julius," the key phrase of his main job, was apparently just a code message to him.

Gold at this time in 1945 had been interested in communism for twelve years; he had been a spy for ten.

After a period of hardship during the depression, Gold got a job with a soap-manufacturing company in Jersey City through a friend named Tom Black. Black, a Communist, had singled Gold out as a good Party prospect. One of the few close friends Harry Gold ever had, Black also introduced him to many new acquaintances.

Gold's loyalty to Black was such that in April, 1935—just ten years before this fateful spring—he agreed to "keep his eyes open" for new chemical processes which might be passed to Black and, by him, to channels that would take them to Russia.

Physically, Gold was the right man for purposeful obscurity: he had a most "forgettable" face. Even Klaus Fuchs, who was to know him well and under extraordinary circumstances, could not remember him. Later when he was cooperating with British Intelligence, Fuchs said he honestly could not remember what Gold looked like.

Gold had a bland moonface. He was neither slender nor fat, neither handsome nor ugly. At thirty he already had his discouraged, slouched shoulders and was outwardly far more mouse than man, shy, quiet, always neatly but never sharply dressed. On a May night in 1945, Harry Gold went to a table in the rear of Volk's Café, near 42nd Street and Third Avenue, in New York. There he met a man named Yakovlev, who had been his immediate superior in the spy machine since March of the previous year. This was the same Yakovlev who, in June, 1944, had arranged for Gold to meet a Dr. Klaus Fuchs, in Woodside, Queens.

Now, in 1945, Yakovlev told Gold that he would be sent on a trip West within a few days, to meet Fuchs again. On this trip Gold would be known as "Dave of Pittsburgh." He would go to Santa Fe, New Mexico, and meet Fuchs. Then he would go to Albuquerque and pick up some drawings from a Los Alamos scientific technician, "Mr. X," whom we now know was David Greenglass. Gold's password would be, "I come from Julius."

Gold was nervous about the entire project. Just traveling across the country was quite a thing for this shy man. "How will they know me?"

From his pocket Yakovlev took one half of an ordinary Jello box-top and gave it to Gold as his recognition device. The other half had already been given to David Greenglass by Julius Rosenberg, his brother-in-law. Neither half had any markings on it, other than the printing one would expect to find on a piece of box of raspberry Jello. Julius

Rosenberg reportedly said of this idea, "The simplest ideas are the cleverest."

Sunday morning, June 3, less than a hundred days to the time when the bomb would be ready, Harry Gold walked up a steep flight of stairs in a second-rate apartment building at 209 North High Street, Albuquerque, New Mexico.

A young Army Corporal, officially T/5 David Greenglass, opened the door. He was only twenty-three but a big chunky man, bigger and better-looking than Gold.

"Mr. Greenglass?" asked Gold very softly. "Julius sent me," he added, after Greenglass uttered a noncommittal "Oh."

At that, Greenglass let him into the room, walked over to a table, and picked up his wife's purse. Taking out his piece of the Jello box, he walked silently back to his visitor. Gold produced his part of the label. They did not need to bring the two pieces into actual contact; it was perfectly clear that they matched.

Gold said, "I'm Dave from Pittsburgh."

Greenglass told Gold that he had some information but that it would have to be written out. They had been expecting him, but not on that particular day. Gold would have to wait. Returning to the Hotel Hilton, he went to his room and read a mystery story for several hours. Had anyone wanted to, they could have located him easily, for he had registered under his right name. This was one of the two mistakes he made on that trip.

In midafternoon Gold went back to North High Street and found them waiting for him. Ruth Greenglass had made tea and provided some cookies. Greenglass was now in his Army uniform, and his manner was much more businesslike. His report was finished, neatly done on 8-by-10-inch ruled white paper.

His drawings showed ways of making bomb "lenses," which helped to focus the superexplosions. These lenses, like the Dragon or the Guillotine, were part of the answer to the matter of timing—in millionths of a second.

At that time the first bomb had not yet been tested—but Los Alamos was already at work on the plutonium bomb, which was to supercede the uranium bomb.

Greenglass was only a machinist, and reports as to his competence varied, then and later. Julius Rosenberg sometimes told him he was no good at all. But on those sheets of paper Greenglass had caught the essential mechanism of the final instrument produced by genius. He and Gold, of course, did not have to fully understand, they only had to fulfill their mission to transmit these drawings.

Gold became very nervous. He could not get away fast enough. The Greenglasses, who had not been out of the apartment all day, insisted on walking with him toward his station. He insisted that they drop him when he reached the USO building. When they reached it, Corporal Greenglass and his wife went into the building, and Gold kept on walking.

The night of June 5, Harry Gold arrived back in New York from his trip to New Mexico.

Through various subway trips, Gold traveled a zigzag route, performing stunts that pleased him and that perhaps on the right occasions would have been useful. For example, he waited, apparently reading his newspaper with great concentration, until the doors of a subway car were about to close. Then he jumped up and got off the train at the last minute. Thus he traveled to a quiet neighborhood far out in Brooklyn, where Metropolitan Avenue runs into Queens.

His appointment with Yakovlev was set for 10:00 P.M.

They saw each other in the distance and approached each other cautiously. At the last moment either of them might see something that would lead him to avoid the meeting. In that case, they would pass with no sign of recognition. But tonight things went smoothly: Brooklyn and the entire world seemed asleep and unaware of these two quiet men.

They met; they greeted each other quietly; they walked together for a block—and they exchanged newspapers.

The paper given by Yakovlev to Gold was empty. But in Gold's newspaper were two large Manila envelopes. One envelope was marked DOCTOR and one was marked OTHER. They contained the information from Klaus Fuchs and David Greenglass.

Perhaps two minutes elapsed. Then the two men separated hurriedly.

Scientists, and others, would differ bitterly about the precise importance of the drawings in the envelope marked OTHER, but not that the whole transaction gave the basic concept of an improved version of the bomb that was yet to be made. When Yakovlev walked off with the envelopes, facts and ideas on an improved bomb passed into Russian hands.

10.

The British and the Russians

EARLY IN JUNE, Colonel Tibbets was told that he would have a working model of "The Gimmick" not later than August 6. To Colonel Tibbets and the 509th, the time was Bomb Day minus sixty.

On the night of June 5, President Truman invited Joseph E. Davies, Fleet Admiral William D. Leahy, James F. Byrnes, and Acting Secretary of State Joseph G. Grew to dinner at the White House.

Davies had just returned from a trip to see Churchill, whom he found in a state of great agitation. One May night at Chequers, his country home, Churchill had kept Davies up nearly all night. From eleven o'clock until four-thirty the next morning they had reviewed the world situation and the Prime Minister's fears for the future.

Churchill told Davies, "Perhaps it will fall to a very few men to decide in the next few weeks the kind of life that will confront several generations to come."

This conversation was crucially important to United States foreign policy, for Truman at that time was learning the inside story of our relations with our wartime allies.

All of the men present at dinner had been special friends of Roosevelt, and Truman had the greatest respect for their judgment.

Mr. Grew had been Ambassador to Japan at the time of Pearl Harbor; Mr. Byrnes at this point was a private citizen and member of the Interim Committee. Davies had been Ambassador to the Soviet Union, but on this occasion had returned from an unusual diplomatic mission to England.

Truman had asked Davies to sound out the Prime Minister on a ticklish subject: Since Truman, as Senator and Vice-President, had never met Premier Stalin nor gone to any of the wartime summit meetings, he thought that it might be appropriate for him to have a separate meeting with the Russian dictator—before the forthcoming meeting of the Big Three.

According to Davies, Churchill had reacted emotionally and most unfavorably to this suggestion, although he was strongly in favor of the Big Three Conference, already tentatively planned for a month later, at Potsdam.

Davies told Leahy and Truman that, in general, the Prime Minister was tired, nervous, and working under great stress. Churchill was also fed up with Charles de Gaulle, the leader of the Free French, and bitter toward Marshal Tito, whom he thought to have placed Yugoslavia completely under Stalin's thumb. Davies said Churchill was "vehement and violent" in his criticisms of the Soviet Union. He thought that the secret police and Gestapo methods in the areas the Soviets had occupied were "more horrible" than communism itself.

Leahy felt that Churchill's highly emotional state did not

augur well for discussions "with the cool, implacable Stalin who probably would face us across the conference table."

But the White House dinner guests could not disagree with Churchill's sentiment that "perhaps it would fall to a very few men to decide in the next few weeks the kind of life that would confront several generations to come."

Churchill was quite disturbed because America was withholding atomic secrets from England. Keeping a watchful eye upon allies, as well as upon the enemy, was second nature to Churchill. And, although Truman could not be expected to be fully aware of it, the British had been on the inside of atomic secrecy at the outset of the project—five years before.

At the beginning, when scientists on both sides of the Atlantic were first excited over the scientific discoveries of Meitner, Hahn and Strassman, Fermi and Szilard, the British and Americans had been full partners. It had been decided that the American side of the Atlantic would be the safest place to build the production plants. Moreover, it was agreed that, although Americans would do the major part of the engineering and the atomic production centers would be in the States, scientific talent and all useful information would be in a common pool. It had also been agreed that neither nation would use a bomb without consent of the other. This had all been set out in personal meetings between FDR and Churchill, at a Quebec conference and a Hyde Park meeting.

As the war went on, the Churchill temper had flared out more than once over whether the British were being consulted in policy matters and getting their share of facts.

When Churchill was ill in February of 1943, after the Casablanca Conference, doctors described him as the world's worst patient. He was "restive, cantankerous and constantly calling for the forbidden cigars." At the time of this illness Churchill had time to do a lot of thinking about the atomic bomb.

At Casablanca he had expressed his concern to Harry Hopkins, then personal adviser of President Roosevelt, and Hopkins had promised to look into the subject of atomic secrecy.

On February 16 of that year Churchill irritably cabled Hopkins: "I should be very grateful for some news about this, as at present the American War Department is asking us to keep them informed of our experiments while refusing altogether any information about theirs."

A few days later Hopkins cabled back for more information, "since I gather the impression that our people here feel that no agreement has been breached. . . ."

From his sickbed Churchill dashed off more cables, one of them a complete chronology of all Anglo-American dealings on the subject. Churchill said, "Urgent decisions about our program depend on the extent to which full collaboration between us is restored . . ." He added that this was so serious, Britain might have to go it alone—and that, he said, would be a "sombre decision."

The main American view of this was that the project had passed from the research phase to the actual design and manufacture of a weapon. To a great extent, then, the operating control was all the further from the hands of civilian scientists—who are traditionally believers in free information and international exchange—and securely in the hands of military men.

At this juncture Vannevar Bush, the key figure in American military research, wrote to Hopkins that information would be supplied to British scientists on the usual military need-to-know basis. He said, "There is nothing new or unusual in such a policy." The need-to-know rule says that a person, even when fully cleared for secrets, is not given secrets wholesale. He is not given a blank check, so to speak, but must establish that the information he seeks is needed by him for furtherance of the military mission.

It was not easy then (nor is it now) to attack the need-to-know rule. But scientists say it is something like telling a prospector, "We will give you a shovel when you know precisely where you wish to dig." A scientist often has to dig a little here and there, until a sixth sense tells him he has hit a likely spot. Some scientists, both British and American, worked throughout the war without feeling a need-to-know about the atomic bomb; therefore they were never told.

This interpretation of the policy—by Bush, General Groves, and others—considerably reduced Britain's scope as a partner in the atomic enterprise. It gave her limited military information and more general scientific knowledge, but expressly prevented her from receiving data of "application to non-war and post-war matters," to use Bush's words.

The British objection, as Robert Sherwood put it in *Roosevelt and Hopkins,* was that it "gave the United States exclusive possession of all the fruits of joint research including the possible use of atomic energy for industrial purposes after the war." There was not too much Britain could do about it at the time.

This policy remained the subject of much friction between the Allies and was not settled by the end of the war —or for years afterward. The policy was an outgrowth of plain physical fact: the laboratories and production plants were here, and the sources of the new knowledge, instruments and scientific brains were here. The enterprise was secret, but the Churchill-FDR agreements were even more secret. To most of the people working on the project, this was an American enterprise, and that was all there was to it.

Thus it was that the various committees considering the use of the bomb hardly gave a moment's consideration to the British position in the matter; much less did they think, as Franck and his colleagues had suggested, that the United Nations might be consulted. There is barely a line in the record to show any consultation with the British.

There was an Anglo-American committee, the Combined Policy Committee, which supervised atomic affairs, but it was not an avenue for consultation or decision on grand strategy. The British technical adviser to this group had merely reported to his government on April 23 that "it was as certain as such things can be" that a weapon would be ready by late summer.

A few days later another member of the Policy Committee, Field Marshal Wilson, informed London that "the Americans propose to drop a bomb sometime in August." This would be a curious use of words by one member of a full and complete partnership, in reporting on something which was technically a joint action. But it conforms with how Americans later viewed "their bomb."

About three weeks after Stimson had briefed President Truman, Anthony Eden was in Washington, and on May

14 Stimson informed him of work on, prospects of, and plans to test, the atomic bomb.

It appears strange that Churchill was not more fully consulted about, or impressed with, the approaching tests. He complains in his own account that he was not fully informed—or else that he had forgotten that a test was coming off. Admiral Leahy says that he found Churchill at Potsdam not nearly so well informed and alert as usual. It must be recalled that during this period, Churchill's hands were full of troubles on the domestic political front, and that campaigning and a subsequent election were being forced upon him.

The lack of consultation between partners does not seem so strange if one concludes that, to a great extent, military use of the bomb was a foregone conclusion. Stimson's actions and memos indicate many reservations about the method by which the bomb might be used, and they also indicate a great reluctance to use it. But he himself never said that it should not be used at all, and he later wrote, "At no time, from 1941 to 1945, did I ever hear it suggested by the President, or by any other responsible member of the government, that atomic energy should not be used in war."

Churchill held the general position that the bomb was being built to be used, and he approved it. More than that, he had done what in America would have been unheard of —he had informed his political opposition and had gone over the subject with the Labor party leader, Clement Attlee. Churchill had no searching questions he had not answered for himself, and for his government, about the use of the bomb.

The British were more concerned with the postwar uses

of atomic power. But in Canada, notably at a first-class research center at Chalk River, scientific information was coming into British hands. And the entire enterprise was almost completely dependent upon Canadian uranium. Unless, as seemed unlikely, America discovered unexpected sources of uranium ore after the war, she would, sooner or later in peacetime, have to negotiate most cooperatively.

At his right hand throughout the conflict, Churchill always had a first-class physicist, Lord Cherwell, who interpreted for him the "war of the laboratories," the latest advances which could improve offense or defense. Furthermore, Churchill knew that many topflight British scientists were engaged in collaborative research with the Americans at various atomic centers in Chicago, Oak Ridge, and Los Alamos. Churchill had no reason to doubt that these men would have a complete understanding of what had been done.

Among those who had come from England to our atomic laboratories were James Chadwick, John Cockcroft, William Penney, and M. L. E. Oliphant. There were many more; some to become famous, some to remain unknown—and some to become infamous.

Klaus Fuchs, a naturalized British citizen, was counted as British. At this time he was working in America with a famous physicist, Hans Bethe; they were discussing the theoretical problems of hydrogen-fusion. We have noted that another young British scientist who worked on the atomic project was Alan Nunn May. It must be remembered that more than a year before Davies and Churchill had their all-night talk, in April of 1944, Nunn May had delivered a sample of uranium to his superiors in the Russian spy apparatus.

This was part of the background for the approaching conference of the Big Three, in which each of the three victorious allies could not escape some feeling that the other two were getting information not openly discussed among the Three. These suspicions, we can see, were correct; all three were deceived in some degree.

However, as far as military secrets were concerned, it was the British who complained to us. The Russians did not complain.

On the morning of June 13 the President had breakfast with Leahy and Davies, and again they went over some of these matters.

Before breakfast the President had written a chatty letter to his mother and sister:

> Dear Mama & Mary: It is just two months last night since I took the oath of office—and what a two months! The next two years can't hold any more. I don't dare think of facing the next two months let alone two years. I have to take things as they come and make every decision on the basis of the facts as I have them and then go on from there; then forget that one and take the next . . .

Describing the day ahead of him, he wrote:

> I am having breakfast with Mr. Hopkins, Mr. Davies, and Admiral Leahy this morning to discuss Russian, German, Italian and British affairs. It ought to be an interesting breakfast and maybe a headache—you never can tell . . .
>
> It is rather lonesome here in this old barn without anyone. . . . I am all alone . . . Went to bed at 11:30 after

> reading dispatches, letters, reports, etc. The clocks have all decided it's seven o'clock. One with a hoarse voice leads off . . . then comes the gold clock on the bedroom mantel . . . the ship's clock in Mrs. Wallace's room bangs away in that crazy sailor count of bells. And then the old grandpa clock in the hall comes out with the high squeaky voice you remember . . .

Three days later Mr. Truman wrote Mama & Mary again:

> Monday I entertain Eisenhower, a real man. Tuesday I go to Olympia, Washington—Saturday a week from today San Francisco, Sunday back here, Monday June 25th appear in the Senate and Wednesday 27th Independence, 28th K.C., and home for a few days and July 3rd Governors' Conference at Mackinac, Michigan and then get ready to go to Berlin. How would you like to be the President *des Etats Unis?* It's a hell of a life . . . love to you both . . .

In this schedule, "San Francisco" was then the home of the United Nations; "Berlin" was a reference to the coming Big Three Conference; and June 18 was the day of a meeting of special significance in this story. At this meeting, almost by accident, the policy-makers of this country were startled by the potential of the atomic bomb.

11.

"Plans for the Japanese Invasion"

ONE LOVELY JUNE DAY the American captains and kings met to consider one topic: how to defeat Japan. On June 18 President Truman called his Joint Chiefs of Staff to the White House, to review invasion plans for the Japanese homeland. The Chiefs, the military heads of the services, had met on June 14 and 15 to consider the outlines of operations which, in this planning stage, were OLYMPIC and CORONET. The strategy, as it was then developing, was to give up our "island-hopping" policy, which meant fighting the Japanese almost hand-to-hand from one island to another. The new plan was to strike with all our might at the main Japanese islands.

Secretary Stimson was pleased to note that civilian advisers were present at this Joint Chiefs' meeting, a return to the procedure that Franklin Roosevelt had abandoned in 1942. President Truman, it might be recalled, had served in the first war in uniform, and was a great admirer of many military men. At this time he had the greatest respect for General Eisenhower, and he often described General George C. Marshall, who presided over the Joint Chiefs, as "the greatest living American." However, President Truman, by his statements and record, was a firm believer in the American tradition of the direction of the military enterprise by firm civilian control. Truman this year was reading and rereading books and histories on the structure and philosophy of the American form of government, and his decision to bring some civilians to the Joint Chiefs' meeting was neither casual nor impulsive.

As it happened, this change in the make-up of the meeting had an interesting result. One of the civilians invited was John J. McCloy, who was serving as Assistant Secretary of War. McCloy was aware that the previous Commander-in-Chief had not paid as much attention to the principle of civilian direction, and in McCloy's opinion this sometimes resulted in grave oversights. If war is a continuation of politics by other means, McCloy reasoned, then one still ought to keep civilian political objectives in mind as one wages war. In other words, the Assistant Secretary of War on this particular day was thinking that military methods and military considerations had come to dominate national and foreign policy, and that it was time, and past time, for a better balance to be restored. Acting Secretary of State Grew was not present at this session. But McCloy was thinking of "State angles" more than of the War Department's mission, narrowly defined.

McCloy has written that he felt that "Mr. Grew for some time had been most energetically urging a political approach to the Japanese, but his thoughts never seemed effectively to have gotten to the White House, at least prior to the June meeting."

The session was called to decide upon major strategy to bring about a Japanese "surrender," and that strategy was seen as a military decision for the Commander-in-Chief. Should we concentrate our attack on the home islands of the Japanese? In McCloy's account,

> After the President's decision had been made and the conference was breaking up, an official not theretofore participating, suggested that serious attention be given to a political attempt to end the war.
>
> The meeting fell into a tailspin, but after control was recovered, the idea appealed to several present. It appealed particularly to the President. . . .
>
> It was also at this meeting that the suggestion was first broached that warning be given the Japanese of our possession of the bomb before we dropped it. Although all present were "cleared," the uninhibited mention of the "best-kept secret of the war" caused a sense of shock, even among that select group.
>
> All present in the room knew that the scientists and engineers working on that project had given definite assurance that within a very short period of timc an atomic explosion embodying military consequences of great significance would occur.

Did they really have word of this "great significance"? This statement is one of the few that indicate the high command had received—and also believed—assurances that the bomb would work. We have seen the assurances given to the Interim Committee, but reports had been in "channels" long before that.

In January, as the highest diplomatic and military representatives of the United States prepared to go to Yalta for a Big Three meeting, a special report on atomic energy had been prepared by General Groves for Secretary Stimson and General Marshall. At that time General Groves had predicted (correctly) that a bomb would be ready by August and another before the end of the year—and others at shorter intervals thereafter. Later Groves was to say he had also held the opinion that two bombs would be all that were needed to end the war.

Then why didn't the weapon figure more in strategic thinking? Perhaps secret records could tell us, perhaps not; but two reasons may be deduced from the visible record. For one thing, Groves' estimate (to Marshall), dated December 30, 1944, predicted (incorrectly) that the first projectile would have an effect equivalent to 500 tons of TNT, and the next one would be twice that. The first in fact turned out to be equivalent to forty times this estimate, namely, 20,000 tons. Unless the military planners were quite close to the Project, they were only given reason to think it was a spectacular improvement in bombs, not another kind of warfare.

Then, too, some of the highest military leaders, who had reason to be more correctly and currently informed, simply could not quite believe their ears.

McCloy mentions this skepticism and other reasons for the trend of the discussion on this particular day.

> Now this incident indicates that, at that time, everyone was so intent on winning the war by military means that the introduction of political consideration was almost accidental. . . . Not one of the Chiefs nor the Secretary thought well of a bomb warning, an effective argument being that no one could be certain, in spite of the assurances of the scientists, that the "thing would go off."
>
> As a result of the meeting, a rather hastily composed paper was drawn up. It embodied the idea which later formed the basis of the appeal to the Japanese to surrender. . . . It

> is interesting to speculate whether, better prepared, this proposal might not have included statements of the policy which we put into effect in Japan almost immediately after the war ended. Such a proposal might well have induced surrender without the use of the bomb. . . .

Truman's recollection of this day centers upon the proposal made by Grew earlier (see Chapter 7) for a surrender proclamation to be sent to Japan. Truman at this point does not discuss the idea of telling the Japanese they could keep their Emperor.

As Truman saw it in retrospect, Grew called upon him, that June 18, to favor sending a proclamation at once or in a few days, when the Okinawa battle would certainly be over. The service chiefs wanted to wait until later. Truman himself made the decision that the proclamation would be issued from Potsdam, to "demonstrate to Japan and to the world that the Allies were united in their purpose."

Truman wrote later that he had thought

> by that time, also, we might know more about two matters of significance for our future effort; the participation of the Soviet Union and the atomic bomb. We knew that the bomb would receive its first test in mid-July. If the test of the bomb was successful, I wanted to afford Japan a clear chance to end the fighting before we made use of this new-gained power.

Further on the subject of the military-political relationship, it may be noted that on this day of June 18th, General Eisenhower returned to the United States capital for a triumphal parade. He rode before the greatest crowds in

Washington's history and delivered a speech to a Joint Session of Congress.

And to complicate matters, we may note that the bomb was *not* uppermost in the minds of military men. The Joint Chiefs at this time had to be reminded by a civilian that the bomb was coming. And secrecy and perhaps lack of imagination kept them skeptical about its "going off." For example, the President's personal Chief of Staff, Fleet Admiral Leahy, remained skeptical until the last as to whether it would work at all. Admiral Leahy on June 4, had received a special "briefing" from a civilian, James F. Byrnes.

Byrnes had the bomb very much on his mind after the Interim Committee meeting, and he went to Leahy's home to discuss it.

Leahy's main reactions were first that he did not believe that such a bomb could really be made, and secondly, that he personally did not approve of mass bombardment. A scientist had told the Admiral that he hoped the bomb would not work. Leahy hoped so, too, and the wish was father to the thought. The Admiral had had a long experience with explosives, he had specialized in gunnery, and at one time headed the Navy's Bureau of Ordnance. So he had some reason to trust his judgment. This bomb did not fit anything he knew about explosives.

The Admiral said bluntly that he regarded mass bombardment as "against the civilized laws of war," and he added, "These new concepts of 'total war' are basically distasteful to the soldier and sailor of my generation."

Leahy was the final link in the chain of command and advisers to the White House: The command links followed the sequence—Oppenheimer, civilian director of the bomb project—to General Groves—to Secretary Stimson—to the President, whose personal military adviser was Admiral Leahy.

Following this meeting of June 18, the Secretary of War was directed to prepare a proposal of policy toward Japan. Naming him to this task was another indication of the interwoven military-political threads in our wartime American government. Mr. Grew, our most recent Ambassador to Japan and Acting Secretary of State at this time, was not asked to draw up this basic document, even though he had had years of experience in dealing with the Japanese and his agency was the one that was supposed to formulate broad policy toward other countries.

Stimson himself was a former Secretary of State, and he had firsthand knowledge of Asia. Many years before this, he had been the father of our policy toward Japan—and in fact toward all nations we judged to be aggressors. In 1945 it had been Stimson's assistant, McCloy, who had the original idea for a political approach to Japan. There could have been many reasons for entrusting this assignment to this old eagle.

Stimson had lived a long time and had a long view of history. He knew the military viewpoint and some of its assets and weaknesses. Stimson knew Asia and understood some of the fundamental facts about the great world outside America. As a politician he said of his Philippine experience that he knew he had "to avoid even the appearance of racial snobbery." That seemed easy for him. He and Mrs. Stimson opened the doors of the Governor's residence, and its social affairs, to the natives, in a manner they had never seen. Stimson did not think of Asians as different and not human beings like ourselves.

It was a logical choice for Truman to ask Stimson to organize a thoughtful approach to the Japanese. And from the point of view of the atomic bomb, the main factor was that Stimson had lived with it for years.

Stimson and his assistant McCloy set to work immediately. In World War II Stimson had been responsible for conducting regular meetings among representatives of the War, Navy, and State Departments, to achieve better understanding and more unified action. A preliminary draft of his memo on Japanese policy was discussed at such a meeting on June 26. Six days after that it went to the President.

As had been said, in the discussion with the Joint Chiefs Stimson reasoned that the approach to a Japanese surrender had to be made *after* a great show of strength to Japan—but *before* we sent any invading force to Japanese soil. He concluded that the Japanese will-to-fight would not diminish, but indeed would be stronger for some time to come, *if* we landed soldiers on her home shores.

Stimson's arguments—which were of course the subject of much staff study in the Pentagon—started with this idea, also pointing out that a landing operation would be "a very long, costly, and arduous struggle on our part." He said that "the terrain, much of which I have visited several times, has left the impression on my memory of being one which would be susceptible to a last-ditch defense, such as has been made on Iwo Jima and Okinawa, and which of course, is very much larger than either of those two areas."

His basic conclusion on the merit of a political approach was that it would be "well worth while our giving them a warning of what is to come and definite opportunity to capitulate." He said that "the warning should be given in ample time to permit a national reaction to set in."

In his memorandum to the President, the mood of the times was such that Stimson felt it useful to say:

> Japan is not a nation composed wholly of mad fanatics of an entirely different mentality from ours. On the contrary, she has within the past century shown herself to possess extremely intelligent people, capable in an unprecedentedly short time of adopting . . . the complicated technique of Occidental civilization. . . . Her advance . . . has been one of the most astounding feats of national progress in history . . . I believe Japan *is* susceptible to reason in such a crisis to a much greater extent than is indicated by our current press and other current comment.

Stimson felt that the timing of this warning message to Japan was most important. He also urged that it must carry a double message: a promise of destruction if rejected, and a promise of hope if she surrendered. He thought everything depended upon the *potency* of the warning, and he cautioned that Japan seemed to have "an extremely sensitive national pride." The wrong words might increase her desperation, with hideous results for both sides.

For many reasons Stimson was in agreement with Grew and others who believed that we should offer Japan a peace which would enable her to keep her Emperor. He did not argue with their observations as to what this would mean to Japan. But he knew what such an apparent reversal of policy would mean to the United States. On the issue of keeping the Emperor, he said it was his *personal* view that "if we should add that we do not exclude a constitutional monarchy under her present dynasty, it would add substantially to the chances of acceptance." Stimson stated more strongly, however, that we should make clear that we did not have as a goal the destruction of the Japanese as a nation, nor the extirpation of the Japanese as a race. Yet, he said we should "express our determination to destroy the authority of those who deceived and misled the country into embarking on world conquest."

In keeping with the nature of atomic secrecy at that time, this memo did not even mention the atomic bomb. And it must be understood that, two weeks before Potsdam and four weeks before it was dropped, the bomb was *not* a major consideration in the Pacific War. Stimson said that work toward this surrender policy was begun, not at all *to avoid use of the bomb* but because of a desire *to avoid invasion,* if at all possible. Various intelligence estimates that spring and summer talked of a half-million, a million, or more lives to be lost in such an amphibious operation.

The particular military situation at any given time was always in the forefront of the thinking of Stimson and his advisers. He and they had been directly opposed to Grew's conciliatory position as late as May, before the battle for Okinawa was over, because they felt that any conciliatory statement then might be considered a show of weakness. Stimson later was to write, ". . . in war, as in a boxing match, it is seldom sound for the stronger . . . to moderate his blows whenever his opponent shows signs of weakening . . ."

Personally, he thought that we ought to negotiate with

the Japanese about keeping their Emperor, but still he felt that "it was not the American responsibility to throw in the sponge for the Japanese; that was one thing they must do for themselves." If they had indicated to the United States that they were willing to surrender, Stimson would have urged negotiation to soften "unconditional surrender." But, Stimson felt that the peace feelers and the intelligence reports of the day could not possibly be interpreted as meaning that Japan wanted to surrender.

Meanwhile, the secret weapon that was the fruit of the work of Fermi, Szilard, and those who followed them was in a strange way emerging from the laboratories and approaching the international stage, where the issues it raised would converge on the issues already causing men so much blood, sweat, and tears.

On June 19 Harry Gold took the Flushing subway as far as it would go to keep another appointment with his espionage chief Yakovlev, who told him that the envelopes, DOCTOR and OTHER, that he had turned over on June 5 had gone to Moscow and were judged to be "extremely valuable."

On June 20, as Stimson in Washington worked on his memorandum, the Japanese Emperor, in Tokyo, called the six members of his Supreme War Direction Council and told them it was necessary to have a plan to end the war at once, as well as a plan to defend the home islands. The War Council, militant and defiant, told him they saw no reason to spend energy upon surrender plans. In the absence of any conciliatory word from us, this meeting did not do much to guide the Japanese toward surrender.

But it was one of several indications, some known to the Allies at the time, that can be looked back upon as evidence supporting those United States leaders who counseled that it was time to change our policy of unconditional surrender.

With no word from the Japanese indicating a softening of their attitude, our Joint Chiefs of Staff met again in Washington on June 29, and approved general plans for the invasion of the main Japanese island, Kyushu. The plan was called Operation OLYMPIC and was scheduled for November 29. In the following spring, in March, there would be an invasion of the island, Honshu. That plan was called Operation CORONET. Yet the Chiefs also sent word to the Pacific command to do some planning for another contingency—namely, that the enemy might collapse suddenly!

Also in late June, the inner circle in Washington was bothered by a newspaper story that originated in London. Commander Herbert Agar, an aide to the American Ambassador, was quoted as saying that *the Germans would have succeeded in splitting the atom by August 6.* Our Office of Censorship was asked to kill the story, but decided that was impossible. Censorship, however, did ask all editors not to expand this story nor try to develop new angles. The story disappeared and has apparently been unremembered from that day to this.

Also from London, more basic news was forthcoming through secret channels.

Churchill has written, "British 'consent to the use of the weapon' was given on July 4." (The British who handled the message on that day doubtless did not notice that it was the anniversary of American independence.)

After this consent was given, as Churchill solemnly puts it,

> The final decision now lay in the main with President Truman, who had the weapon; but I never doubted what it would be. . . . The historic fact remains, and must be judged in the after-time, that the decision whether or not to use the atomic bomb to compel the surrender of Japan was never even an issue.

Apparently this was a bridge for which Mr. Churchill had long been ready.

12.

The Last Minutes

BY SOME OTHER MEN, of course, the bridge of decision had not yet been crossed. Some felt close to a decision, but were not quite ready to cross. Others did not have the power to decide, but felt they still had the power of speech to influence those responsible. In this latter class were a number of scientists, the most active of whom was Leo Szilard.

As we have noted, this man had not made a lasting impression on James F. Byrnes. It is perhaps significant that when Byrnes wrote his memoirs, *Speaking Frankly,* he did not even mention the visit that Szilard paid him, nor did he refer to anything that Szilard wrote in the memo given him at his home on May 28. But Szilard was still busy. He had worked on the Franck Report, and now he had one more thought—a petition.

This scientist, like Stimson, thought "the bomb was mostly considered from the point of view of its possible use in war . . ." But in his letter to Roosevelt, delivered by hand to Byrnes, Szilard said, "The years which will follow can be expected to be far more important . . ." and he thought they would be dangerous to the United States. In June and July,

Szilard was still talking, insofar as security would let him and others would listen.

He had warned in his letter that the bombs then being made would be *much less powerful* than those "we know could be made." He thought Russia could soon duplicate our atomic effort. He thought our long coastline would make us vulnerable to bombs smuggled in, or fired from offshore submarines. And he warned of guided missiles:

> . . . if there should be great progress in the development of rockets after this war, it is conceivable that it will be possible to drop atomic bombs on the cities of the United States from very great distances . . .

Szilard thought that the basic strength of the United States had been in its production ability—we were winning a war because of our capacity to make things in large numbers. This superiority-through-production now belonged to the past. Massive production ability would not be the decisive factor in the next war, Szilard reasoned.

Szilard, like Franck, thought about the atomic arms race, which might start with the announcement of our dropping of a bomb; this would lead to a competition with Russia, which would lead to consideration by both sides of "a preventive war."

Szilard also discussed some of the technical factors in setting up any international atomic-control system. In his general conclusion of the May letter to Byrnes, he said that our policy ought to be directed toward achieving such a system of control . . . "before the next presidential elections . . ." (Szilard was not a political scientist).

If atomic control were set up, he concluded, "we would

then perhaps have a chance of living through this century without having our cities destroyed."

Leo Szilard, in 1939, had done some of the decisive experiments proving that neutrons were emitted during fission. Hence, a chain reaction could be sustained. Szilard had long ago turned this weapon around, so to speak, in his mind, and he could see the shape of the bomb *as it looked when coming toward you.*

Szilard tried to get these considerations before those who could act upon them. As Compton said much later: "There were few who sensed as clearly as did Szilard the shock that would be felt throughout the world if the atomic bomb destroyed large numbers of Japanese lives." Again, in Compton's words, "the case against use of the bomb in the Japanese theater was pressed most vigorously by Leo Szilard."

After the trip to Washington and to Carolina to see Byrnes, Szilard circulated petitions around the atomic project at Chicago, while sympathetic colleagues circulated similar ones at Los Alamos and Oak Ridge. This was an extraordinary thing to do on the site, or around the fringes, of a super-secret Army project.

In the first form of the petition he circulated, Szilard said that once the bombs were used it would be difficult to resist the temptation of using them again, and "thus a nation which sets the precedent of using these newly-liberated forces of nature for purposes of destruction may have to bear the responsibility of opening the door to an era of devastation on an unimaginable scale."

According to Compton the petition in this form found

"almost no support." Then, according to Compton, the petition was rephrased so as to approve the use of the weapons "after giving suitable warning and opportunity for surrender under known conditions."

Szilard gave this petition, representing the views of sixty-seven scientists, to Compton, for delivery to Washington, sometime in the middle of July. The petition and the names disappeared into secrecy—and they are still locked somewhere, safe from the eyes of enemies or friends.

Counter-petitions were also made up by other scientists. One statement for a military use of the bomb said: ". . . these sentiments, we feel, represent more truly those of the majority of Americans and particularly those who have sons . . . in the foxholes and warships in the Pacific." Another, addressed to the President, was close to Stimson's line of thinking. It urged that the bomb be dropped only *if* the Japanese had been given a chance to surrender with hope of peaceful development as a nation, and *if* convincing warnings had been given that a new weapon would be used and—an extra provision—*if* responsibility for the use of atomic bombs were shared with our allies. (According to McCloy, Stimson in June felt strongly that a clear warning should be given to the Japanese.)

Compton and General Groves thought these statements and counter-statements made it difficult to get an idea of how the people on the atomic project felt about use of the bomb. Therefore, Oppenheimer at Los Alamos, Ernest O. Lawrence at Berkeley, and Farrington Daniels, then director of the Chicago Metallurgical Laboratory, were asked to report on how scientists in their respective laboratories felt about this weapon.

Oppenheimer and Lawrence were able to report on this at the Scientific Panel meeting mentioned earlier. Their report, also signed by Compton, noted a wide difference of opinion.

Daniels, at Chicago, decided to conduct a poll of 150 scientists. He knew that it was not being conducted according to the rigid standards a social psychologist would have used. Therefore, Daniels referred to the group he surveyed by the scientifically correct term, "a random sample."

The polling was voluntary and informal, and all who were asked voted. There was only one question: *Which of the following procedures comes closest to your choice as to the way in which any new weapons that we may develop should be used in the Japanese war?*

Of the five possible answers given with the question, one may be dismissed, for only 2 per cent of the scientists voted for it—that was to keep the whole business secret and not use the weapon at all. This thought, which ordinarily occurred first to military men, had always seemed impossible to most scientists. They gave as the main reason that what we had learned by asking questions of the atom, others could learn.

The four alternatives, then, and the percentage of the poll *voting for each* as their choice, in the order of their popularity, went like this:

Give a military demonstration to Japan to be followed by a renewed opportunity for surrender before full use of the weapons is employed.

For a Military Demonstration: 46%.

Give an experimental demonstration in this country, with representatives of Japan present: followed by a new oppor-

tunity for surrender before full use of the weapon is employed.

For an Experimental Demonstration, with Threat of Use: 26%.

Use them in the manner that is from the military point of view most effective in bringing about prompt Japanese surrender at minimum human cost to our armed forces.

For Military Effectiveness: 15%.

Withhold military use of the weapons, but make public experimental demonstration of their effectiveness.

For Withholding Military Use: 11%.

The results of this poll also were locked in secrecy for years, and when released long after the war they touched off bitter criticism of Compton by other scientists.

In this poll, physical scientists were attempting what social scientists know to be a far more involved procedure than it appears—the design and administration of a questionnaire. Every word is important in its design—a fact that a psychologist must know, but that a physicist is likely to ignore. For example, what is meant by *a military demonstration?* Was the German bombing of Coventry a military demonstration? Was Hiroshima?

Interpreting the results of this questionnaire has caused many an argument among some of the famous scientists concerned. The poll was historically important, for it had been officially requested, and it received an official interpretation, as we will see.

It can be seen that only 15 per cent wanted the weapon used as military efficiency dictated. That means that 85 per cent had reservations, according to one way of reading these results.

The alternative that got the largest vote, 46 per cent, was to give a military demonstration, but *not* "full use," for it assumed there would have been previous opportunities to surrender before full use of the weapon.

The number who wanted to withhold military use, 11 per cent, and the number who wanted to have an experimental demonstration over here first, 26 per cent, add up to 37 per cent. If one assumes that by *military demonstration* before "full use" the respondents did *not* have in mind a bombing of a civilian population, one can add that 46 per cent to arrive at a figure of 83 per cent being opposed to first use of the bomb in any ordinary way, i.e., as bombs were used upon Coventry, London, Hamburg, Berlin, and the other bombed cities.

As Compton read this poll, he reached almost the opposite conclusion, for in his own words he summed this up as follows: ". . . there were a few who preferred not to use the bomb at all, but 87% voted for its military use, at least if after other means were tried this was found necessary to bring surrender."

Compton has said that his "experience with this questionnaire has confirmed my faith in the reliability of democratic processes in judging matters of human concern." In his judgment, "the same points of view . . . with closely the same degree of relative frequency . . ." were found in three different groups of men consulted in the course of these few weeks. He was referring to the Interim Committee, to scientists and other scholars, and to the mechanics in the shops of the Manhattan Project.

There was little time left for further explorations of opinion. The poll was forwarded to Washington, and Compton said an "immediate reply" was received, showing that it was being considered. By whom?

Daniels took his poll on July 12. That was just twenty-five days before Bomb Day, the hour when "The Gimmick" would be ready for the plane. Men were working around the clock at Los Alamos, in the center of the desert, and at Tinian, in the center of the Pacific. And there was another event that seemed to have outpaced the chances of scientists' opinions being heard any further.

The President and his principal advisers were already on their way to Europe for the Potsdam Conference. They had departed the weekend of July 6, a week before the poll was taken.

Any further call from political power to the laboratories would have to be made at the eleventh hour.

Yet in fact *that call did come,* once more the phone would ring. But time was running out—with the bombers, with the men in the desert, and in the Berlin that bombers had made into a desert.

On the night of July 12 a team of scientists and technicians from Site Y went to the testing site called Trinity. In an old ranch house they worked on the final assembly of their delicate electronic device.

Their motions were expert. Much of this was like a story they had read before. But they worked quietly and tensely. Radiation cannot be seen or felt by man's senses, so even after years of familiarity a man feels a certain jumpiness when close to possible exposure. This has to do with danger, and also with importance. Simple instruments can give clear signals when they are near the unseen presence, and simple rules will prevent accidents. In fact, accidents with radiation have been quite rare.

In this case, the final assembly was new to them, as would be the end result of these practiced familiar motions. No men in the world had ever put together a device quite like this one; only these men had ever put together the separate parts.

As one familiar sub-assembly was brought into place and made ready, as the pieces were joined to each other and began to look like the dreams, the drawings, and the nightmares, a sigh would go up, or a self-conscious joke. Would all of this fit together and check out on time? There were only three nights left before test day.

At one point the pressure focused entirely upon the brains and hands of Dr. Robert F. Bacher, the theoretical physicist who was in charge of the vital heart of the device:

One component definitely did not fit at the time it was brought to its place. This was unbelievable! Parts had been machined to the extremes of precision and measurement; they fitted perfectly. Now, on this component, surely no one could have made an error?

Bacher judged this lack of fit to be a matter of expansion or contraction due to temperature changes: one piece of metal was slightly warmer than the other. The crew waited three minutes, listening in the desert night to the sound of their watches—and their hearts.

After waiting for the temperatures to equalize, they tried again, and the outer piece of metal slid effortlessly to join the other. With a few more adjustments the assembly would be complete.

The assembly crew, dead-tired, were still nervous, and did little clean-up tasks.

On Saturday, the night of July 14, the entire unit was raised to the top of a steel tower, which stood in the center of nowhere, like a crude machine-age altar, waiting for a secret ceremony.

This raising of the unit to its resting place had also been well rehearsed. They had even hoisted a dummy device to the top of the tower a few days before—a fake containing ordinary explosives—but not meant to explode or fire.

But it had fired when lightning struck it! That had not been planned in any rehearsal: no one had counted on anything but man-made lightning.

All that weekend men came and went with their trucks and jeeps, their black nonmagnetic hammers, their various needles and threads to make new patterns. They carried probes and "sniffers," oscilloscopes and portable ionization chambers. They trailed long cables like snakes across the sandy earth. And they wired the device with delicate nerves; it would send out information up to the last moment.

Then the device was as ready as it would ever be.

13.

Tinian: "The Glory Boys" Make Ready

SIX THOUSAND MILES from San Francisco, men of the 509th continued to build up their Pacific base.

The island of Tinian, then containing the largest airfield in the world, is about the size of the island of Manhattan, which it somewhat resembles in shape. With wry GI humor, the streets and areas of the Tinian installation had accordingly been named as Fifth Avenue, 125th Street, and so on, in the same general relationships as their New York counterparts.

In the neighborhood of Times Square (on Tinian) there were to be twenty-one raised tents to house the sleeping quarters of the technical experts.

In upper Manhattan was the airfield from which the B-29's were taking off on practice missions. In ordinary operations from the Marianas, thousands of men would take off in one armada—and the 509th men, who watched the planes come home in the night, thought it one of the grandest and strangest sights in the world.

But on their own practice flights the men of the 509th went over the Pacific and (after July 20) over Japan with only three planes. Each crew might comprise thirty men, who had already known each other and worked together for months.

Among the officers were Colonel Tibbets, Major Thomas W. Ferebee, Captain T. J. "Dutch" Van Kirk, and Major Charles Sweeney. Among the men were Sergeant Joe Stiborik, Master Sergeant "Nails" Kuharek, a Regular Army man and flight engineer; Sergeant Abe Spitzer, radio operator; Staff Sergeant "Buck" Buckley, also known as "Muscles," a radar operator; Al "Pappy" Dehart, a Texan and a tail-gunner; Roy Gallagher, an assistant flight engineer and, at twenty-three, the youngest of them all.

These men were used to each other, and chafed at making further practice runs. These men, except for Tibbets, did not know the purpose was not only to give them training but to get the Japanese antiaircraft gunners used to the idea that three B-29's could fly over without bringing hundreds more in their train. The high command, naturally, did not want the plane carrying "The Gimmick" to be shot down at all, but if it were brought down and lost its bombload before it reached the target, the consequences could be extremely serious. Secrecy would be lost—and, moreover, there would not be a supply of bombs, for each one was virtually made by hand.

The bomb had still not arrived at Tinian, and the waiting added to the nervousness of the outfit. The men of the 509th sometimes found it difficult to pass the time: they had played poker, drunk PX beer, and read comic books until they could not bear the sight of them.

The air crews also found that the ground crews, arriving first, had managed to give others at Tinian the impression that this particular outfit had the final superweapon that would end the war. Some of the other outfits on Tinian were flying over thousands of miles of ocean, risking the fire of hundreds of enemy weapons every week. These combat veterans did not take warmly to the new, green outfit, fresh from the States, which was said to have a special hot-shot magic.

The other outfits on Tinian enjoyed ribbing the men of the 509th, whom they dubbed the "Victory Boys" or the "Glory Boys."

A GI poet eventually turned out an entire ballad aimed at them. The song was called "Nobody Knows":

Into the air the secret rose.
Where they're going, nobody knows.
  Tomorrow they'll return again.
But we'll never know where they've been.
  Don't ask us about results or such,
Unless you want to get in Dutch.
  But take it from one who is sure of the score.
The 509th is winning the war.

When the other Groups are ready to go,
  We have a program of the whole damned show.
And when Halsey's Fifth shells Nippon's shore,
  Why, shucks, we hear about it the day before.
And MacArthur and Doolittle give out in advance.
  But with this new bunch we haven't a chance.
We should have been home a month or more,
  For the 509th is winning the war.

This came under the head of good, clean fun, but there were more sinister jokes in the air.

The Japanese radio began making fun of the 509th. The

propaganda radio called them by their right number and said their secrecy was ridiculous.

Abe Spitzer and his buddy, Roy Gallagher, would hear of Tokyo Rose's latest insinuation about the "magic" of their outfit—and they would wonder how the news ever got to Tokyo from Tinian. It was enough to keep a man awake at night.

Still alive, far "back in the woods" on Tinian, perhaps with radio equipment, there were Japanese who had not surrendered. What motives kept the Japanese going? What would happen when "The Gimmick" was dropped?

Men like "Muscles" Buckley and "Pappy" Dehart did not have the answers. When they lay awake, they wished they did have the answers.

Meanwhile the Glory Boys tucked away in their foot lockers, as souvenirs, their mimeographed copies of the song, "Nobody knows."

As I look back over the five years of my service as Secretary of War, I see too many stern and heart-rending decisions to be willing to pretend that war is anything else than what it is. The face of war is the face of death; death is an inevitable part of every order that a wartime leader gives. The decision to use the atomic bomb was a decision that brought death to over a hundred thousand Japanese. No explanation can change that fact and I do not wish to gloss it over. But this deliberate, premeditated destruction was our least abhorrent choice. The destruction of Hiroshima and Nagasaki put an end to the Japanese war. It stopped the fire raids, and the strangling blockade; it ended the ghastly specter of a clash of great land armies.

In this last great action of the Second World War we were given final proof that war is death. War in the twentieth century has grown steadily more barbarous, more destructive, more debased in all its aspects. Now, with the release of atomic energy, man's ability to destroy himself is very nearly complete. The bombs dropped on Hiroshima and Nagasaki ended a war. They also made it wholly clear that we must never have another war. This is the lesson men and leaders everywhere must learn, and I believe that when they learn it they will find a way to lasting peace. There is no other choice.

—Henry L. Stimson, *On Active Service*

14.

"Terminal": The Big Three Enter Einstein's World

LOOKING FOR a place to meet, the victors of the war had not been able to find suitable rooms and quarters in the Berlin they had blasted to bits. Thus, the meeting, with the code name of TERMINAL, convened the middle week of July in the suburb of Potsdam.

Long before that meeting, Potsdam had been home to two famous men of the twentieth century. One was the Crown Prince Wilhelm. He had maintained an establishment there, chiefly used for relaxation, the Cecilienhof Palace. It was a building of moderately bad and moderately grand architecture, with formal gardens where a man could conduct discreet conversations—for political or personal purposes. It was here the Big Three held their conference, the last of the wartime conferences, the terminal "summit meeting" of the series, Quebec, Teheran, Yalta.

This old city for many years had also been the residence of Albert Einstein. Along the shady streets, he had walked, as he later walked at Princeton, with his dog and his thoughts running ahead of him, and his pipe smoke lingering after him.

Einstein loved the peace of *his* Potsdam. Here, on his fiftieth birthday, he had received what seemed like presents and cards from the entire human race. The Professor and his housekeeper had sat on the pleasant porch, sorting the birthday mail into vegetable and fruit baskets and hoping to answer the letters as time would permit. Less than a year after that, Einstein had been forced to flee Germany into exile.

Over the weekend of July 14, 1945, the Big Three Conference arrived, the largest conclave of world leaders ever to meet in the Palace of Potsdam. They were the first statesmen ever to meet in Einstein's world.

By the time of Potsdam, the high command of the United States and Britain were looking well beyond the immediate military situation, to the shape of the postwar world. They were concerned about creating some kind of stable peace —and they already felt that their main problem was and would be their relation with Russia. As described by such participants as Churchill, Truman, Robert Sherwood, Averell Harriman, Joseph Davies, and the historians McGeorge Bundy and Herbert Feis who had access to the original records, the troubles with Russia had begun before Roosevelt's death and were acute by the time of Potsdam. The accounts are quite clear and unanimous: Russia was the main concern of most of the farsighted statesmen at that time. Only occasionally did anyone link the problem of Russia with another new problem coming into the world.

Jonathan Daniels does attribute one rather flippant line to Mr. Truman. The former Presidential assistant, in his book about Mr. Truman, states that before the bomb was tested, and therefore before Potsdam, Mr. Truman remarked one day, "If it explodes, as I think it will, I'll certainly have a hammer on those boys."

These colloquial words sound like the man from Missouri, but they do not fit other statements by the President at that time, nor statements made later about this Potsdam period. And one cannot find elsewhere in Mr. Truman's statements any hint that he anticipated the Alamogordo test and strongly assumed the A-bomb would work. Truman made this flip remark before Potsdam.

The records otherwise indicate that only Stimson and McCloy, among ranking civilians, believed in the bomb, and that ranking military officers were either skeptical or indifferent.

As we will see, Stimson at Potsdam did write a paper on Russia and the bomb. One might think that officials would have done this sooner. After all, Professors Franck and Szilard had thought about the relation of the USSR to the uranium bomb. But high officials at that time did not seem to have the information or the time to think about these things.

The prevailing mood among our delegation going to the Big Three Conference was one of sober responsibility toward their problems, but the bomb was not one of them—although the tragic spectacle of bombed Berlin deeply impressed all who saw it.

Stalin was late in arriving for the opening of the conference, scheduled for Monday, July 16, so President Truman took advantage of the time off to visit Berlin.

He rode about in an open car with Admiral Leahy and

James F. Byrnes, whom he had just appointed Secretary of State. Both advisers have written about their views of the wrecked city and the profound impression the rubble of destruction made upon them and the President.

Said Leahy:

> Every building we saw was badly damaged or completely destroyed. This great and beautiful metropolis . . . was wrecked beyond repair. One of the stops we made was before the smoked walls of the Reichschancellery, from the balcony of which Hitler had screamed his orations to hordes of obedient Nazis. . . .

The President, noted Admiral Leahy, commented on the error of a nation turning back to barbarism and expecting to get away with it. "It is a demonstration of what can happen when a man overreaches himself," the President remarked. "I never saw such destruction. I don't know whether they learned anything from it or not."

The remark stayed in Leahy's mind during the two-hour tour. And perhaps he was thinking, as he often did in those days, of himself as a young midshipman, when he sailed around the Horn in the old *Oregon* and saw his first bombardment during the battle of Santiago—there he had seen civilians bombed by the U. S. Navy at Guantanamo Bay.

As the Admiral watched the long lines of civilian refugees fleeing the Russian-occupied areas in the East, he found it "an acutely distressing spectacle . . . witnessing the progress of a great world tragedy."

That night, as he reported it, the President's personal party discussed the end of the war without any mood of vindictiveness or revenge, but with a new realization: "To those who had fought the war in Washington . . . there was a new realization of the horrible destructiveness of modern conflict."

The next day the delegations plunged into the intricacy of modern diplomatic conflict. They met in a former palace reception room large enough to permit all the principals to sit at a round table. Through the windows they could see the landscaped gardens the Hohenzollerns loved. Flags and uniforms of the three nations, and the spirit of victory, added color to the conference.

But the meetings were to be full of differences and dangers. The Western powers hoped to decide on a policy toward Germany and Italy. They also had to discuss Soviet policies in the occupied areas, and Stalin wanted to talk about the disposition of German ships, and about reparations. He was also to raise the possibility of some overseas territories for Russia: the USSR wanted to own certain territories, to be like the Western countries in that respect. Russia also wanted to eliminate the Free Polish government. Stalin also was to raise the question of Spain and Franco: the Spanish government, he felt, had been imposed on its people by Germany and Italy. Now that the dictators were vanquished, what about Spain?

Potsdam was tremendously burdened with power politics and with equally thorny practical problems.

Russia was scheduled to enter the war in the Pacific in accordance with the agreements made at Yalta. She and the United States and Britain at that time faced great military transportation and morale problems; war commanders were asking men who were veterans of Europe to travel around the world and fight in "another war."

The lights burned late in the Cecilienhof Palace and in the Western delegations' headquarters in nearby Babelsberg.

Back home the lights were also burning late in Washington—and in New Mexico.

There is, of course, a difference in time between Potsdam and Washington. It was Monday, July 16, in Europe—but Sunday night, July 15, in the United States—when an officer of the Office of Censorship received a dramatic telephone call at his home in Washington. The Security Office of "manhattan" was on the line.

Certain key people in Censorship had been told a few details of the atomic project, in order that they could intelligently watch for any leakage, any break of the story of "manhattan." Now a security officer was tipping off Censorship to be on the alert. This phone call was to keep certain censors wide awake all that night. Conceivably there might be a disaster. Something might cause a panic. Or a radio commentator might see something he could report. If so, the story perhaps could still be stopped before it went out on a network.

A Colonel William A. Consodine was saying to Lieutenant Theodore Koop in Washington:

"Something is going to happen in New Mexico at daybreak tomorrow."

In New Mexico, that night began with rain and lightning.

The men of Los Alamos looked at the tower from time

to time, and could sometimes see human figures on top the tower as jagged flashes in the sky outlined silhouettes. Then the figures would be lost again in the blackness and the wet. Since the dummy had accidentally been touched off, protective devices against lightning had been installed. But men were still jumpy when the lightning flashed. One young scientist became hysterical and physicians ordered him removed from the scene.

Time and again Oppenheimer and the others stepped out of their bunker to ask themselves whether the sky was getting lighter. Four o'clock in the morning was test time. The equipment was ready and 500 miles of wires were waiting for their signals. But the bad weather caused one postponement after another.

All around the site of Trinity the desert stretched away, and intermittently the workers could see the mountains, a darker black in the weather.

The only inhabited locality near the site was the village of Carrizozo, where 1500 persons lived and, at the moment, were sleeping. The town was thirty miles due east of Ground Zero, but the scientists had worried about radiation. Army trucks stood ready to invade the village at a moment's notice, if wind conditions became dangerous. The soldiers were to rush into the town and awaken the townspeople in the middle of the night. Their orders were to rouse every one—men, women, and babes in arms—bundle them into the trucks and rush them to safety.

At 5:30 A.M., the command knew the soldiers did not have to disturb this American village.

In later times men did not speak of the noise, but of the light:

General Thomas Farrell wrote:

> *There came this tremendous burst of light.*
>
> The whole country was lighted by a searching light with the intensity many times that of the midday sun.
>
> It was golden, purple, violet, gray and blue.
>
> It lighted every peak, crevasse, and ridge of the near-by mountain range with a clarity and beauty. . . .

Since light travels more swiftly than sound, first you see light, then you hear the sound. Even so, men were surprised and shocked as they watched, lost in the changing configurations of light and vapor, which some imagined were like convolutions of a giant brain.

The real shock came when the noise reached them a few seconds later. They had forgotten there would be a roar.

The noise woke up Carrizozo. In the dark, sleepy men and women sat up in terror, asking, *"What was that?"* And some, through their windows, saw a pillar of fire, six miles high, in the dawn. What was it? But there was no one to answer their questions.

Secretly a message carried over the 500 miles of wire was condensed into three words designed to wake up men at Cecilienhof Palace. A Signal Corps man at Potsdam tore it from the teletype: "BABIES SATISFACTORILY BORN."

On July 17, Potsdam time, Churchill had a visitor from the American delegation: "Stimson called at my abode and laid before me a sheet of paper on which was written, 'Babies satisfactorily born.' " Stimson explained that this meant the bomb test had come off. Churchill considered this to be "world-shaking news."

The next morning, as Churchill recalls, they all received "a full description of this tremendous event in the human story." (The supplementary material also came in code. For example, it was said that "the babies' cry" could be heard at Leesburg, and the "light in babies' eyes" seen at Highhold. Translated, this meant if the bomb had dropped in Washington, D.C., the sound could have been heard at the Virginia home of General Marshall, and the flash would have traveled as far as Stimson's home on Long Island.)

Churchill's response was one of exultation:

> To quell the Japanese resistance man by man and conquer the country yard by yard might well require the loss of a million American lives and half that number of British—or more, if we could get them there: for we were resolved to share the agony. Now all this nightmare picture had vanished. In its place was the vision—fair and bright indeed it seemed—of the end of the whole war in one or two violent shocks. . . . The Japanese people, whose courage I had always admired, might find in the apparition of this almost supernatural weapon an excuse . . .

He mentioned another aspect of the weapon: the West would not need the Russians in the Pacific, and would have no need to ask favors of them.

And it was true that high American officials had no enthusiasm for Russia's entry, at this late hour, into the Pacific war. To Churchill, a better bargaining position with the Russians meant that European problems could be faced on their merits. He wrote in later times, "We seemed suddenly to have become possessed of a merciful abridgement of the slaughter in the East and of a far happier prospect in Europe."

Thus, it is no exaggeration, though it may be an irony,

to state that to Churchill the first light of the Trinity bomb seemed to spread sunshine on all sides of the globe. Very shortly, however, Churchill was to speak more grimly about the "secrets of the atom, long mercifully withheld from man."

On the day after the news, questions about use of the bomb did not exist for Churchill, but "a more intricate question" was what to tell the Russians.

On July 18 Churchill discussed with President Truman the question of the extent to which Premier Stalin should be informed of particulars about the weapon. The Prime Minister did not propose that he should be told at all. Churchill on that day informed his Cabinet that the President "seemed determined to do this," and the Prime Minister added, "I replied that if he were resolved to tell, it might well be better to hang it on the experiment, which was a new fact . . . therefore, he would have a good answer to any question 'Why did you not tell us this before?' "

Churchill also noted that Truman had a firm resolve to give no details in any conversation with Stalin.

(It might be further noted that during the war the Allies had made frequent complaints about the secrecy of their Russian ally. The Soviets gave the Western powers nothing like the general information on new or old equipment that the Soviets ordinarily received from the West. There had even been incidents over the fact that the West was not allowed to follow the usual custom of sending observers to see how Western equipment which *we had furnished,* had worked out on the Russian front. There were serious complaints to the effect that we could not even get information about our own weapons.)

On the 18th, Mr. Truman held a meeting with several of his principal advisers to discuss the Conference and the important news.

Besides talking to General Marshall and Admiral Leahy, Truman consulted with Byrnes; General Arnold, Chief of Staff of the Air Forces; Fleet Admiral Ernest E. King, Chief of Staff of the Navy; and "others."

General Dwight D. Eisenhower, Commander-in-Chief of the combined forces in Europe, also came to Potsdam and was informed by Stimson of the new weapon. But General Eisenhower was not, in his own words, "an official witness or advisor." He "expressed the hope that we would never have to use such a thing . . . take the lead in introducing into war something as horrible and destructive . . ." Like General Marshall, General Eisenhower also had the thought that if the weapon could remain secret, it would be better for the world. Since the General had never before had any kind of briefing on the bomb, his reactions were, as he said, "personal and immediate . . . not based upon any analysis of the subject."

Other persons were present, according to the President, but their names did not appear in any public official accounts. What each adviser said may be inferred from their attitudes as written elsewhere, but minutes of this meeting are not available to the historian.

In this conference, on the 18th, the President essentially agreed with the recommendations of the military, that the bomb should be used—unless an ultimatum to Japan should produce the desired surrender without it. As Truman has written, "I then agreed to the use of the atomic bomb if Japan did not yield."

The President also agreed that the "wheels should be set in motion," the operational machinery made ready, so that the planes could take off, if so ordered. But according to a letter written by Truman, he still held "the final decision in [his] hands." He was not yet ready to cross his bridge of decision.

In *Mr. President,* the scrapbook of memoirs he wrote with William S. Hillman, Truman has said of this day, "I wanted to weigh all the possibilities and implications. Here was the most powerful weapon of destruction ever devised and perhaps it was more than that." He put his feelings into two short sentences: "It was not an easy decision to make. I did not like the weapon."

The President's advisers, likewise, failed to share Churchill's first optimism and enthusiasm for the bomb.

James F. Byrnes, who had listened to the arguments of Leo Szilard and also of the various members of the Interim Committee, was now Secretary of State. His view, as he recalled it later, was: "No one who played a part in the development of the bomb . . . felt happy about it . . . I have no doubt that all thinking men in the armed forces felt the same way . . . the truth is, war remains what General Sherman said it was." (Sherman said, "War is hell.")

Admiral Leahy was the most vehement of all about mass bombing. To use such bombs, he thought, was to adopt "an ethical standard common to the barbarians of the Dark Ages . . . I was not taught to make war in that fashion . . . these new and terrible instruments of uncivilized warfare represent a modern type of barbarism not worthy of Christian man."

And what was Stimson, the man upon whom the President most depended, thinking?

Compton, who saw Stimson both inside and outside of the Interim Committee meetings that spring, has said that he seemed bothered by "after-thoughts." The Interim Committee had made a firm recommendation to Stimson—and to the government. But the Secrctary had not stopped thinking and reflecting. In fact, for years to come Stimson was to keep on asking himself questions about the various alternatives.

While at Potsdam, Stimson wrote down some of his conclusions for the President to ponder—insofar as the President could ponder anything while under the stress of the Potsdam meeting.

Stimson thought that the two great problems of the postwar world were Russia and the bomb. He linked them together in his thinking at the Conference and in the paper he wrote for the President.

At Potsdam, most members of the American delegation were, personally as well as politically, depressed by their first intimate experience with the secret and nonsecret police methods of the Soviets. Not only the goals of the Soviets but their methods of operation seemed quite different from ours.

In his memo Stimson expressed this feeling very strongly, and concluded, ". . . every effort we make at permanent organization of such a world composed of two such radically different systems is subject to frustration by misunderstandings arising out of mutual suspicion."

He further suggested that it would be particularly difficult to set up a control system for atomic weapons in cooperation with any totalitarian country. In fact, he personally thought it would be impossible; effective control of the new force could not be managed by any organization "containing as one of its dominant members a nation . . . controlled by the autocratic machinery of a secret political police."

Therefore Stimson wrote that "before we share our new discovery with Russia we should consider carefully whether we can do so safely under any system of control . . ."

But to Stimson, as to the generals and the admirals, the dominant and immediate fact was the war.

Their intelligence estimates (which later proved to be correct) stated that the Japanese still had a well-equipped army of five million men. Our General Staff estimated that slightly under two million were in the home islands; two million more in Korea, Manchuria, China, and Formosa; and another million in scattered locations. The Japanese Navy, on the other hand, was in poor condition, while we were ready to employ the most powerful naval forces ever assembled.

We also had superiority in the air, and virtual control of the air over Japan. Yet no one could write off the Japanese planes and their kamikaze pilots. If the Japanese chose to fight to the end, the General Staff estimated as of the middle of July that "the Allies would be faced with the enormous task of destroying an armed force of five million men and five thousand suicide aircraft, belonging to a race which had already amply demonstrated its ability to fight literally to the death."

Against these forces, in the operations called OLYMPIC

and CORONET, the Allies planned to send equivalent forces—five million men.

"We estimated that if we should be forced to carry this plan to its conclusion, the major fighting would not end until the latter part of 1946, at the earliest [and] cost over a million casualties to American forces alone," Stimson wrote.

But would the Japanese fight to the bitter end? Intelligence did not have the final answer, any more than did the men on Tinian.

To Stimson, it would have been wrong to guide the policy of the war toward a main goal of avoiding the use of the bomb. It would have been equally wrong, he thought, to guide policy in such a way as to make sure the bomb had to be used. As he saw it, the goal, as far as this weapon was concerned, "was the use of the atomic bomb in the manner best calculated to persuade . . . the Emperor . . . to submit to our demand for what was essentially unconditional surrender . . ."

Stimson felt that the Japanese Emperor should have a compelling reason for surrender and "the reason furthermore must be of such a nature that his people could understand his decision." To Stimson, "the bomb seemed to me to furnish a unique instrument for that purpose."

In what Churchill called "the after-time," Stimson was to raise many questions, based on hindsight: Could we not have been more explicit about the weapon? Could we not have been explicit about letting the Japanese keep their Emperor? Were the judgments of the intelligence experts seriously mistaken about the Japanese attitude toward surrender? These questions were all considered before Potsdam and, as we shall see, the Potsdam Declaration was to show that one set of answers was made for the whole world to see.

What did Stimson later think of the actions decided on? He felt that criticism should not start with the bomb, as policy did not start or end with it. There could have been several alternatives, several different approaches to ending the war and securing Japanese surrender. But the bomb was only an instrument of policy, although he knew it was a revolutionary instrument. But there was a main purpose before all those who worked at Potsdam, and the bomb was "a unique instrument for that purpose."

Stimson's feelings were, in his own words:

> My chief purpose was to end the war in victory with the least possible cost in the lives of the men in the armies which I had helped to raise. In the light of the alternatives which, on a fair estimate, were open to us I believe that no man, in our position and subject to our responsibilities, holding in his hands a weapon of such possibilities for accomplishing this purpose and saving those lives, could have failed to use it and afterwards looked his countrymen in the face.

Thirty days before this, on April 25, the memorandum that Stimson and General Groves took to the White House had said:

> Within four months we shall in all probability have completed the most terrible weapon . . . the world in its present state of moral advancement compared with its technical development would be eventually at the mercy of such a weapon . . . if the problem of the proper use . . . can be solved, we would have the opportunity to bring the world into a pattern in which . . . our civilization can be saved.

Stimson had posed these questions squarely to the new President.

When Truman met with his advisers in Potsdam, it was one day after the first bomb test, three months after he became President, and nineteen days before the bomb and the plane and the weather would be ready.

What was the President thinking at this point? To some extent, we may conclude, he was waiting for events to help him decide. But he seems always to have been absolutely and clearly aware that it was his decision to make.

Truman has written several different accounts of the course of events that led to the decision. They differ somewhat in details, even as to the date on which he first discussed atomic energy, or the date on which he spoke with Premier Stalin about the new weapon. But the accounts are unwavering as to who took the responsibility for using or not using the weapon.

There is not a line in any account of his that implies that the decision was made or mainly influenced by any one person, by the military, the Interim Committee, or by the meeting of advisers at Potsdam. He has sometimes implied that it was an obvious decision, at other times that it was not easy. Both of these answers could be correct, in one respect, because there are obvious decisions which sometimes are extremely hard to make.

In any case, Mr. Truman has never implied that the decision was made in any way by anyone else, nor that this specific decision was mainly influenced by any one person—for example, Stimson. Stimson's judgments, as one goes over the record, seem to have been overwhelmingly influential on main issues, but there is no hint from Truman that, on the bomb issue, he borrowed specific conclusions from Stimson, Leahy, Byrnes or Marshall.

Each of the President's statements on the motive for his decision is also firm: He thought that using the bomb would save lives. He does not speak *positively,* as Churchill did, but, rather, negatively, as the choice of a lesser evil—of these atomic deaths saving the world from other deaths. In *Mr. President* he wrote:

> I gave careful thought to what my advisors had counseled. I wanted to weigh all the possibilities and implications. . . . General Marshall said in Potsdam that if the bomb worked we would save a quarter of a million American lives and probably save millions of Japanese. . . . I did not like the weapon . . . but I had no qualms if in the long run millions of lives could be saved.

Later Truman was to write even more firmly, in his memoirs, *Year of Decisions:* "Let there be no mistake about it. I regarded the bomb as a military weapon and never had any doubt that it should be used."

Yet, there is still a third account, a letter which Truman wrote to answer the specific question: When did he decide to use the bomb? In this letter Truman made clear that the final decision was *not* made by him at this meeting, and we will examine this statement later in this story.

A week was to elapse before Truman sent out an operational order, and that was still conditional, according to the President's statements. Meanwhile, questions about our policy were still being asked in Washington, while the planes of the 509th were flying over Japan.

15.

Rehearsals and Actors

AS NOTED BEFORE, on July 20 the regular combat crews of the 509th began their series of practice strikes over the Empire, as the main islands of Japan were known in the Pacific war.

For seven weeks the command under Colonel Tibbets had been engaged in practice, flying over the Pacific to various points and returning. A plane or two would make, say, a navigation-training flight to Iwo Jima, and bomb Rota on their return. Or they would fly out directly to Rota or Guguan, bomb, and return. The final part of this preparation was in much longer flights, to Truk or Marcus. These men were already trained, even overtrained. Now they practiced everything again under combat conditions, with blue water under them.

After July 20, they made such flights against the main islands of Japan. This involved more distance, more fatigue, and real combat danger. In all, the planes made twelve strikes on four days, with two to six planes going against each target.

For targets they had what were rightly considered leftovers, cities that had not already been thoroughly blasted, and obviously of lesser military importance than those which already had "had it." Over each of these cities of the Empire they dropped a real bomb, but one filled "only" with TNT. This bomb was made in a peculiar shape, designed to fall through the air in the same way that "The Gimmick" would fall. This model was a 10,000-pound projectile, which they called "The Pumpkin." It was pumpkin-colored, but the shape—still secret today—doubtless was not.

In these full-dress rehearsals over Japan itself, they otherwise realistically observed the instructions which would prevail on the Day.

Briefings are not available, but these were the specifications:

> *You will proceed to a rendezvous at Iwo with two other B-29's. Only one plane will carry it.*
>
> *The other planes will carry instruments and photographic equipment. You three will not contact each other, but will maintain the strictest radio silence.*
>
> *Weather observation planes will be returning from over the Empire and the area of the targets. They will not address you directly, but speak as if addressing the base at Tinian. You will naturally take extreme care in hearing their reports. If they are not understood you will not break silence to ask repeat. They will be repeated as prearranged.*
>
> *You will approach the target at a ground speed around 300 mph, and maintain a steady bombing platform at about 30,000 feet.*
>
> *Bombing will be visual. If the city of choice is not clear, proceed at your discretion to another target.*
>
> *As bomb is released, you will immediately turn at a 150-degree angle.*

You must not, repeat, not follow standard bombing procedure by proceeding as usual to fly over the target.

When the device leaves your plane, it will fall in much the same curve as any other bomb. Besides falling downward, it will also fall forward, with the momentum it has from the forward motion of your plane. All bombs do this and we usually fly over their explosion. You will not fly over this explosion.

After bombs away, turn sharply so as not to be over Ground Zero when the device explodes. You may even wish to lose altitude to put more distance between yourself and zero.

In precisely this manner the crews struck at Japanese cities or at pinpoints upon the map. Some targets were points close to the real ones. The planes flew over and dropped "Pumpkins" upon Koriyama, Nagaoka, Toyama, and Kobe. But they never made a practice strike directly at any of the genuine nominations.

Those target cities, however, had already been selected, and their names were soon to be submitted, at Potsdam, for the personal attention of Stimson and Truman. There were five.

At Potsdam the Big Three continued to meet, and the struggle went on for many hours every day. Sometimes the talk was bitter and rude; sometimes ideas were veiled in polite language; sometimes thoughts were too vague—at least in translation—to be understood. Churchill thought this the most unsatisfactory and foreboding of all the historic meetings.

The plenary sessions were held in the grand reception hall; at intermissions one could stroll briefly in the garden.

During the war the Cecilienhof Palace had been a hospital, and the Germans had grown beautiful flowers in the garden. The flowers were already rearranged by the Russian hosts. The centerpiece was a Red Star done in a thousand geraniums, and it was considered very beautiful and impressive.

All during this week, staff members worked far into the night, making drafts of memos and communiqués and working on the main military document to be prepared—an item that became known to history as the Potsdam Declaration. From time to time a page or a paragraph would be brought to the higher-ups and then taken back to the workshops to be polished or perhaps completely revised. And, aside from the work to be done, there were state dinners that, to some, seemed to be interminable. Admiral Leahy was impressed by "the battle of music."

On July 19 President Truman gave the first formal dinner for the delegations. Sergeant Eugene List played the piano, and Stalin so much liked Chopin's Waltz in A Minor, Opus 42, that at his urging the three leaders rose for a toast. They went, glass in hand, over to the pianist and drank a toast to his playing. Admiral Leahy reports that the Sergeant turned white as a sheet when he looked up and saw these three coming toward him.

On the 21st, Stalin as dinner host was determined to outdo Truman and List, so he ordered prize pianists sent in from Moscow, as well as two imposing female violinists. The President whispered to Leahy that he estimated that these ladies weighed 200 pounds each, but he thought they played extremely well. This party lasted until 1:30 A.M., a half-hour later than the American party, although at 1:00

A.M. Churchill tried to get the Western delegations to go home. According to Leahy, Churchill said, "I'm bored to tears, I don't like this music, I'm going home." However, he stayed to the end. After it was over, Churchill muttered to Leahy that he would "get even" with the Big Two.

When *he* was host, on the evening of July 23, Churchill had the full orchestra of the Royal Air Force play loud and long. As Leahy put it, "Churchill, with puckish malice, saw to it that the musicians kept going until 2:00 A.M."

It was at this dinner that Stalin proposed that the next Big Three meeting take place in Tokyo. (Arrangements were being worked out for Russia to enter the war against Japan.) Churchill was surprised that the Russian dictator should make such a proposal without asking that the waiters and orderlies leave the room. A security leak might have enabled Japan to prepare better for Russian attack.

Churchill had placed Truman at his right and Stalin at his left, and in the course of the many speeches and the playing of the RAF band, Churchill had conversations with each of them. He reported that Stalin was "in the best of tempers and seemed to have no inkling of the momentous information the President had given me." Stalin spoke with enthusiasm about the Russian intervention against Japan, and "seemed to expect *a good many months of war,* which Russia would wage on an ever-increasing scale." (Italics the author's.)

Then, says Churchill, a very odd thing happened: "My formidable guest got up from his seat with the bill-of-fare in his hand and went round the table collecting signatures . . . I never thought to see him as an autograph-hunter!"

That was the night of July 23, in Potsdam. The next

day the American high command would go over a large map of Japan: They would check over the real list of suggested targets and make it into the final list, if it was approved.

There were no scientists at Potsdam. The report from James Franck and the poll that Daniels had taken at Chicago were somewhere in the machinery of the War Department. Exactly what had happened to them and how much of an effect they had on final results is still shrouded in secrecy. But it can be said that the scientists' views were not completely overlooked.

On July 23 a long-distance call went to Oak Ridge, where Dr. Arthur Compton was visiting the X-10 laboratories.

Colonel K. D. Nichols was given an urgent message to tell Compton, "Washington wants at once the results of the opinion polls on the use of the bomb."

As Compton tells it in his memoirs, *Atomic Quest,* "The votes and the petitions were by now in my hands. I accordingly wrote out a message summarizing the results as objectively as I could and handed it to the Colonel." He judged scientists would approve use of the bomb in war.

An hour later Washington called again. Colonel Nichols again went to see Compton. "Washington wants to know what you think."

In his book Compton wrote:

> What a question to answer! Having been in the very midst of these discussions, it seemed to me that a firm negative stand on my part might still prevent an atomic attack upon Japan . . .

Thoughts of my pacifist Mennonite ancestors flashed through my mind . . .

But I wanted the war to end. I wanted life to become normal again. I saw a chance for an enduring peace . . .

As Compton remembered it years later, he told Nichols, "My vote is with the majority. It seems to me that as the war stands, the bomb should be used, but no more drastically than needed to bring surrender."

Nichols relayed the message to Washington at once. Until the records are opened we cannot know whether this message was sent to Potsdam. . . .

In Potsdam the next day, July 24, General Marshall of the Army and General Arnold of the Air Force met with Truman and Stimson.

The generals explained the basic bombing plans of the 509th, which had been worked out in Washington by General Groves, General "Toohey" Spaatz, and General Thomas T. Handy, Acting Chief of Staff in Marshall's absence.

Cities on the real list were, in the order of their importance as targets, Hiroshima, Kokura, Niigata, and Nagasaki. The fifth city was Kyoto, and a discussion about it took place. Stimson had personally visited Kyoto many years before. It had military installations, and furthermore was nestled in hills in a sort of cup shape, which made it ideal for destruction by a fireball a mile in diameter. But Stimson knew that it was a city of temples, shrines, and artistic treasures. Truman ordered it struck off the list when Stimson said it was a cultural and religious shrine.

Mr. Truman has written:

> In deciding to use this bomb I wanted to make sure that it would be used as a weapon of war in the manner prescribed by the laws of war. That meant that I wanted it dropped on a military target. I had told Stimson that the bomb should be dropped as nearly as possible upon a war production center of prime military importance.

Truman wrote that the order of selection for the four cities

> . . . was in accordance with the military importance of these cities, but allowance would be given for weather conditions at the time of the bombing.
>
> In order to get preparations under way, the War Departmen was given orders to instruct General Spaatz that the first bomb would be dropped as soon after August 3 as weather would permit.

The reported timing of these various orders, directives, and proclamations has been a sometimes mysterious subject.

The President's account says that the military order to go—from Marshall to the Pentagon, to Spaatz, to the 509th—was dated July 24. The Air Force history published a photostat of the original order prepared in Washington and the date is July 25. This is clarified, very likely, by the fact that a draft existed in Potsdam and was approved, and then the working draft was typed and the action copy prepared in Washington on the next day, the 25th.

But more baffling has been the understanding that the grand strategy was to see if Japan would surrender with the employment of the bomb. Japan was to receive a warning, an ultimatum. That document was made public at Potsdam on July 26. And yet, the day before publication of the Potsdam Declaration, the secret orders for the bombing were already on their way.

Were we determined to use the bomb, regardless of how the Japanese replied? Did we assume that the Japanese would certainly say no?

Here is the full text of the military order, as the President gives it in his memoirs.

TO: *General Carl Spaatz* *24 July 1945*
Commanding General
United States Army Strategic Air Forces

1. The 509 Composite Group, 20th Air Force will deliver its first special bomb as soon as weather will permit visual bombing after about 3 August 1945 on one of the targets: Hiroshima, Kokura, Niigata and Nagasaki. To carry military and civilian scientific personnel from the War Department to observe and record the effects of the explosion of the bomb, additional aircraft will accompany the airplane carrying the bomb. The observing planes will stay several miles distant from the point of impact of the bomb.

2. Additional bombs will be delivered on the above targets as soon as made ready by the project staff. Further instructions will be issued concerning targets other than those listed above.

3. Dissemination of any and all information concerning the use of the weapon against Japan is reserved to the Secretary of War and the President of the United States. No communique on the subject or release of information will be issued by Commanders in the field without specific prior authority. Any news stories will be sent to the War Department for special clearance.

4. The foregoing directive is issued to you by direction and with the approval of the Secretary of War and the Chief of Staff, U.S.A. It is desired that you personally deliver one

copy of this directive to General MacArthur and one copy to Admiral Nimitz for their information.

/s/ Thos. T. Handy
General, GSC, Acting Chief of Staff

The bomb material, however, had not yet arrived at Tinian. The 509th had no bomb at that moment—only "The Pumpkin."

But the point is the same: was this the final order? Was the 509th merely waiting for the bomb and clear weather over one of the four cities?

This question troubled the historian of the Army Air Forces, Professor J. L. Cate, when he was preparing an account of the atomic bombers for publication in 1953. He wrote the former President about it, and we will look at that answer a little later on.

On this day of July 24, the President was taking another step that concerned all of the Big Three.

He was going to tell Stalin of our new weapon.

At the end of the day, as the conference broke up, Truman approached Stalin. There are several eyewitness accounts of their very brief encounter. To some, the scene was something like the breakup of the Cabinet meeting on the night of Roosevelt's death, when Stimson lingered at the side of the new President. To others, the meeting was reminiscent of the end of a certain Joint Chiefs of Staff conference, when Mr. McCloy made the startling mention of a new political approach to Japan and the use of the weapon.

Churchill, who said that he knew what was going to

happen and who stood about fifteen feet away, said that after the meeting was over, the group stood about in two's and three's before dispersing. The President went up to Stalin, and spoke to him alone—except for interpreters.

"What was vital to measure was its effect on Stalin," said Churchill. "He seemed to be delighted. A new bomb! Of extraordinary power! Probably decisive to the whole Japanese war! What a bit of luck!"

Churchill said that this was his impression at the moment, and he was "sure that he had no idea of the significance of what he was being told . . . if he had had the slightest idea of the revolution in world affairs which was in progress his reactions would have been obvious."

What *was* he being told?

Truman gives the subject three sentences:

> On July 24 I casually mentioned to Stalin that we had a new weapon of unusual destructive force. The Russian Premier showed no special interest. All he said was that he was glad to hear it and hoped we would make "good use of it against the Japanese."

Churchill spoke to Truman as people returned to their cars. "How did it go?" he asked.

"He never asked a question," said Truman.

The President and Byrnes rode together back to the "Little White House" at Babelsberg. By Byrnes' account:

> He said he had told Stalin that, after long experimentation, we had developed a new bomb far more destructive than any other known bomb, and that we planned to use it very soon unless Japan surrendered. Stalin's only reply was to say that he was glad to hear of the bomb and he hoped we would use it. I was surprised at Stalin's lack of

> interest. I concluded that he had not grasped the importance of the discovery. I thought that the following day he would ask for more information about it. He did not. Later I concluded that, because the Russians kept secret their developments in military weapons, they thought it improper to ask us about ours.

Churchill felt that if Stalin had understood, "nothing would have been easier than for him to say 'Thank you so much for telling me about your new bomb. I, of course, have no technical knowledge. May I send my expert in these nuclear sciences to see your expert tomorrow morning?' "

But it was Churchill who did not understand. Truman had not used the word "atomic." Neither had he used the word "nuclear."

Only the night before, Churchill had been convinced from Stalin's words and manner that he expected Russia's part in the Japanese war to be of considerable duration. The information Stalin received here did not apparently affect him at the time.

Somehow the message, perhaps because of the manner or the words of Truman, apparently did not convey to Stalin the idea that the war might end abruptly and soon. Or one can say, with Byrnes and Churchill, that the blame was in the receiver, not in the transmitter.

This was the manner, then, that something was said about a new weapon as a crowd dispersed. We have seen something like this scene, twice before, when the bomb was mentioned and briefly discussed at the end of meetings which had been called to discuss another subject.

First, when the April 12 Cabinet meeting was over, Stimson stepped up and spoke to Truman, on the night of Roosevelt's death.

Second, when the Joint Chiefs of Staff met, McCloy raised the bomb and the issue of a political approach to Japan.

Now here was the third time, when at the end of a busy Potsdam day, Truman spoke to Stalin.

These were three great left-handed occasions, when the President of the United States heard the news, when the high command was reminded that this weapon might win quick victory, and when one great nation informed an ally of the ultimate weapon.

There may, of course, have been a most ironic twist in this last episode. Stalin may have understood the atomic revolution far better than Truman. Stalin may have had more time to think about it, since his agents had been able to get into Oak Ridge and Los Alamos. Truman, as Senator, had failed to get his investigators into the atomic secrets. Security had stopped the Truman Committee when Fred Canfil was trying to get information at Oak Ridge.

Of course, we do not know for a fact that Stalin was well-informed on the atom. We have seen that it was not easy for scientists to inform governments of the meaning of news from the laboratories. One can only conjecture as to whether the Kremlin listened better to scientists than did the Pentagon.

All observers in July of 1945 were certain that Stalin did not understand. Perhaps Stalin was a convincing actor. It was not until 1950 that the Russian spies Fuchs and Gold were induced to reveal the activities which should have kept Stalin informed.

No one at Potsdam had time to think much about the lack of reaction from Stalin to the news. Perhaps they thought that (like Admiral Leahy) Stalin found it hard to believe in these superweapons. Perhaps, like James Byrnes, he found it hard to understand scientific matters.

On July 24 the order went out, and the "wheels were in motion."

On July 26 the Declaration was issued to warn Japan and to invite her to surrender.

The Potsdam Declaration began with the statement that the governments of the United States, Great Britain, and China, "have conferred and agree that Japan shall be given an opportunity to end the war."

In general, the points in the Declaration grew out of the Stimson memorandum of July 2, which itself had come from McCloy's suggestion.

The Declaration spoke strongly of those Japanese leaders who had "brought the Empire of Japan to the threshold of annihilation." It said, ". . . we do not intend that the Japanese shall be destroyed as a race or destroyed as a nation."

It did *not* say that the Emperor might be kept, but it did say that under occupation by the victors, "freedom of speech, of religion, and of thought, as well as respect for the fundamental human rights shall be established . . ."

The last paragraph of the Declaration contained the final form of the past recommendations that Japan should be warned before the bomb was used. After all the discussion, after all the extremists, at either end, had urged vindictiveness or conciliation, the Declaration itself said:

> We call upon the government of Japan to proclaim now the unconditional surrender of all Japanese armed forces, and to provide proper and adequate assurances of their good faith in such action. The alternative for Japan is prompt and utter destruction.

Did this statement fulfill the recommendations that Secretary Stimson had urged on July 2? The Declaration did not mention secret weapons or surprises. Would it prove to be a warning with *potency*—fulfilling Stimson's admonition that everything depended upon the potency of the warning?

The American delegation, still in Europe, waited anxiously for some reply.

In the timetable of Tinian, it was Bomb Day Minus Eleven.

16.

"Nothing Left To Do"

THE POTSDAM DECLARATION was released on July 26, a Thursday night, and all day Friday the presses and the transmitters of the Western powers beamed it toward Tokyo and announced it to the world in a hundred languages.

Then time was running out—in days and hours.

In Europe, they waited day by day and hour by hour for some answer from the Japanese.

In the Pacific, Colonel Tibbets knew that he could go at any time after the following Friday. From that Friday on, it would be a matter, as it often was with the Air Forces, of "waiting for the weather."

Thus the situation was essentially a time bomb, with fuses running from one end of the world to the other. It was like one of those arrangements which in a gentler age was called "an infernal machine."

The "wheels were in motion"; however, the Japanese could still give some indication of a desire to surrender, and the American high command could still stop the "infernal machine." And the bomb was still not in the Pacific.

Components of it were being sent piecemeal from the States. Some parts went by ship and some by air.

The clock was ticking—no question about that—but accidents and near-accidents could still happen along these lines of communication thousands of miles long.

And accidents did happen.

The cruiser *Indianapolis,* carrying vital components of the bomb, was approaching the island of Tinian. Lightheartedly some members of her crew were writing ribald messages for the Emperor on the casing of the bomb. They did not know what it was, of course; they just knew it was a secret weapon to be dropped by a plane, and GI's often wrote messages on bombs.

The *Indianapolis* unloaded her vital cargo at Tinian on July 26 and then returned to regular duty with the fleet. On July 29, off the shores of Leyte, she was attacked and sunk by the Japanese and virtually all hands were lost. The men who wrote those messages never saw the weapon used in the war. If the ship had been sunk three days sooner, perhaps the bomb would never have been used.

A political accident, which had been kept secret up to this time, was also announced on July 26: The British had held a national election on July 5. Churchill had been campaigning, right up to the time he left for Potsdam. But the results of the election were delayed; they were kept secret while the polling places waited for the mail ballots coming from soldiers overseas. The absentee vote was to arrive, the vote was to be tallied, and the results were to be made public three weeks late. At the meeting Stalin had asked

Churchill how he thought it would come out, and was surprised to learn that the old campaigner was worried, because he did not feel sure of the soldier vote.

Churchill went home from Potsdam on July 25 to await the announcement. His managers were optimistic and he went to sleep reassured. But he awoke at dawn "with a sharp stab of almost physical pain." He felt in his bones that he had lost. He was right. While the Potsdam Declaration was going out on July 26, Churchill at 4:00 P.M. went to Buckingham Palace for an audience with the King, and tendered his resignation. Bitterly disappointed by the defeat, the old man said in a farewell announcement, "I regret that I have not been permitted to finish the work against Japan. For this, however, all plans and preparations have been made, and the results may come much quicker than we have hitherto been entitled to expect."

Mr. Attlee replaced him at Potsdam.

As the news of the Potsdam Declaration and of Churchill's defeat went around the world, preparation of the vital active material for the bomb was still being rushed at Los Alamos.

On the afternoon of July 26, United States time, the last few batches left the plant. They were flown to Santa Fe and then taken by truck to Kirtland Field, Albuquerque, where they were met by three B-29's belonging to the 509th. From there the crews of the 509th took them to Mather Field at Sacramento, arriving on July 28. This was an aerial port of embarkation. The components were to travel from there in the same three B-29's.

One of these planes was called the "Laggin' Dragon," and the flippant name proved to be one of terrible irony.

The "Dragon" had just taken off for Tinian and was only fifty feet up when the life-raft door unaccountably blew open and was yanked loose by the airstream. It wrapped itself around the right control elevator in the tail.

The plane was beyond the runway and was nosing toward the ground. Captain Edward M. Costello and Lieutenant Harry B. Davis, his co-pilot, pulled back on the controls with all their strength, but the big plane fluttered like a torn flag in the wind.

They finally managed an altitude of 300 feet, and the raft fell off the controls. The ground control tower told them that, if they could stay up at all, they should hold out until their gross plane weight was down to 120,000 pounds. All three atomic planes had been loaded to 132,000 pounds, which was a ton more than the absolute maximum ordinarily allowed for the runways at Mather Field.

Staying up, burning up gasoline to reduce weight, was a logical idea. But then Costello noticed they were still in danger. Large areas of the elevator fabric had been torn off, and more pieces were being furled off into the wind. This was really a blood-chilling sight.

Costello had to think swiftly. Perhaps they could make a desperate attempt for altitude—and a mass bailout. But, that would lose the precious cargo. The captain did not know what it was, but he had certainly been impressed with its importance. Yet, a bailout might give the crew a better chance.

Costello went over these alternatives faster than we can now.

The tail began to flutter, the whole ship shuddered.

Costello notified the tower that they would crash-land.

All aboard—except the pilots—assumed the approved crash-landing posture, hands clasped behind the neck, and they held their breath, awaiting the impact of the emergency landing.

To the men in the control tower, the fluttering plane seemed just about to go out of control when the Captain landed her. It was a perfect landing. He did not even have to use his brakes. The special new reversible-pitch propellers had saved the plane, the crew, and the cargo. American technology probably never looked better than it did at that moment to Costello and his crew. But their Pacific flight was delayed, while repair forces took an elevator off another B-29 and replaced the torn elevator of the "Laggin' Dragon."

This kind of delay might have given the Japanese more time. But we cannot say what they could have done with it. In any case, no immediate notice was taken of the Potsdam Declaration by the Japanese. This was quite depressing to the Allies.

When Stalin had arrived in Germany he had brought word that the Japanese, using Russia as a neutral country, had asked him to raise the question of negotiating peace. But Stalin had replied that since the Japanese did not make specific proposals and thus did not give him any concrete proposition to make to the West, he did not see that Russia could do anything. The other Two agreed with him that this was the best answer.

Russia at that time was a neutral in the Pacific war. She was an ally of Britain and the United States in the European war, and was mobilizing herself to declare war upon Japan.

Looking back now, with hindsight, many have thought

we might have done much more with such peace feelers. At the time they were much in the minds of the Potsdam conferees. Byrnes has described how anxiously everyone waited for an answer from Asia. Stimson has detailed his own consideration of all such proposals, and his feeling that ultimately the loser must be the one who takes the initiative, and in no uncertain terms.

Truman felt a deep conviction that we must "show the Japanese we meant business."

Then, on July 28, word came from Japan.

In Byrnes' words:

> . . . we devoutly hoped that the Japanese would heed our warning that, unless they surrendered unconditionally, the destruction of their armed forces and the devastation of their homeland was inevitable. But on July 28 the Japanese Premier issued a statement saying the declaration was unworthy of notice. That was disheartening. There was nothing left to do but use the bomb.

Still, the American delegation hoped that they would have occasion to stop the machine.

Again in Byrnes' words:

> . . . despite the Japanese Premier's statement, I continued to hope the Japanese government would change its mind. I was greatly disappointed when August 2, the day of our departure from Potsdam, arrived, and no further word had been received. I recognized then that our hope of avoiding use of the bomb was virtually gone.

In Truman's words:

> On July 28, Radio Tokyo announced that the Japanese government would continue to fight. There was no formal

> reply to the joint ultimatum of the United States, the United Kingdom, and China. There was no alternative now. The bomb was scheduled to be dropped after August 3 unless Japan surrendered before that day.

However, like Byrnes, Truman still hoped that he would hear some news which would change the situation. Furthermore, he knew that he could still change the directive sent over the signature of General Handy.

When Air Force historian Cate later wrote Mr. Truman about the matter of the order for the bombing going out *before* the ultimatum for surrender, Mr. Truman wrote that he did not consider that directive to be final. Mr. Truman said:

> . . . you raise the fact that the directive . . . is dated July 25th. It was, of course, necessary to set the military wheels in motion, as these orders did, but the final decision was in my hands, and was not made until we were returning from Potsdam. . . .
>
> I ordered atomic bombs dropped on the two cities named on the way back from Potsdam, when we were in the middle of the Atlantic Ocean.

By radio the word was flashed from the middle of the Atlantic to the men who were waiting at Tinian in the middle of the Pacific.

17.

"My God!"

NOW, THE TIME in the Pacific ran in hours and minutes. When the operating command went over the final plans at Tinian, it was decided that Niigata was too far away from the Marshalls; they struck Niigata off the list. Then there were three. They were ranked in the order, Hiroshima, Kokura, Nagasaki.

On Thursday, August 2, a B-29 landed at noon, carrying the last batch of material for the bomb. In all the workshops there and in the plants back in the States, at this time, there had been just enough material for two bombs.

On Friday, August 3, command control shifted to the Pacific—the way was clear, whenever the weather permitted. Weather did not permit on August 3 or 4. Then the word came that skies would be clear on August 5. They made ready to have the bomb aboard that day.

A briefing was held on August 4. In the words of Sergeant Abe Spitzer:

> Colonel Tibbets began by saying that whatever any of us, including myself, had done before was small potatoes compared to what we were going to do now. Then he said

> the usual things, but he said them well, as if he meant them, about how proud he was to have been associated with us, about how high our morale had been and how difficult it was not knowing what we were doing, thinking maybe we were wasting our time and that the Gimmick was just somebody's wild dream. He was personally honored . . . to have been chosen in this raid . . . all the other big wigs nodded when he said it . . . would shorten the war by six months. . . .

Then the intelligence officer spoke:

> One ship will fly to Iwo Jima and stand by in case one of the three strike ships has to abort . . . and oh, yes, the group identity on the tail of your ships will be replaced, and you will not be allowed to carry the name of your ship; that will be replaced by a number, and your call letters will be changed . . . just in case . . . in case anything happens, I mean . . . we can't take any chances . . .

This briefing did, indeed, describe the power of the bomb, but it did not actually tell the crews what "The Gimmick" was. They were not told about atomic energy or about radiation. They were still, in a sense, flying blind.

Some of the crew members had a little time on their hands and walked over to see their planes. Sergeant Spitzer, a radio operator, was anxious and wanted one more look at his equipment. Security guards, however, would not let the men aboard their own planes

Only two men who would be on the mission really understood. The commanding officer, Colonel Tibbets, had been told a good deal about it. The naval officer assigned to the group, Captain William S. Parsons, was a scientist in uniform. He was to assemble the bomb in its final form after the plane took off. He really understood the nuclear bomb, and it would have been considered a disaster to us if he had been captured.

That was very much on Captain Parsons' mind. He did not like what he had heard of torture in prison camps; he feared he might talk. On impulse, just before boarding the plane, the "Enola Gay," he borrowed a revolver from a military policeman. If the plane were forced down in Japanese territory, Parsons could kill himself.

At midnight there was a last-minute briefing on flight plans, air-sea rescue procedure, and the like.

At 0245 on August 6, the "Enola Gay" lifted from the runway. She carried a crew that did not know what was in the bomb bay, a Navy man serving as bombing officer and thinking about possible capture and suicide, and at long last a real bomb addressed to a real city. The two observation planes followed the "Enola Gay" at varying distances.

At Iwo Jima the three planes held a rendezvous and went into precise formation. Then they began a slow climb to bombing altitude—30,000 feet.

At 0730 Captain Parsons and an assistant made the one last adjustment that made *it* into "a final bomb." From then on, everything went exactly like the rehearsals; by this time the 509th already had a "standard operating procedure."

At 0815 they heard from the weather planes. Their orders were to bring the bomb back if all three cities were hidden by cloud. But the weather was sunny and clear. The report on Hiroshima gave excellent visibility.

That was the death sentence. They were just an hour from the city. At 0901 Captain Parsons nervously took a final look at the bomb. At 0911 the ship straightened and leveled into a short bomb run. The controls were passed over to the bombardier, Major Thomas W. Ferebee.

At 0915 Major Ferebee toggled the bomb out, at an altitude of 31,600 feet, ground speed 328 mph.

The plane jumped when the bomb left. Colonel Tibbets again took the controls. Immediately he executed a violent turn. He also let the plane nose downward.

They felt two more *slaps*—shocks that made the plane leap—fifty seconds after the "Bombs Away." The bomb had fallen more than four miles in that time, and had exploded itself, as prearranged, when it reached a height of 2000 feet.

By this time the "Enola Gay" was fifteen miles away. Still the plane jumped twice: *once* from direct concussion from the bomb, and the *second* as "echo" concussion from the bomb bounced back from the earth.

Light filled the sky and filled the plane. In this intense light, every line of the plane's interior stood out as clear as a draftsman's drawing. It made every hair on the back of a man's hand stand crisp and sharp as a needle.

Captain Robert A. Lewis kept a log of the flight; he had been asked to make notes for historical purposes. He wrote, "There will be a short intermission [in the diary] while we bomb our target."

The next entry was: "My God!"

The word was flashed to the high command aboard the USS *Augusta,* in mid-Atlantic. President Truman, exultant at the coming victory, excitedly told the crew, "This is the greatest thing in history."

From the *Augusta,* word went to Washington to release the statements that had been prepared.

And then the world heard the noise and saw the light.

And, like the villagers of Carrizozo, just three weeks before, the world asked, *"What was that?"*

18.

"A Rain of Ruin"

THIS WAS THE beginning of the age we now live in.

Looking back, we tend to remember only the main outlines. The bomb dropped. Japan surrendered. Americans and their Allies celebrated "V-J Day."

But it was not that simple. On the day after the bomb, August 7, 1945, it did *not* seem a foregone conclusion that Japan would surrender because of the new weapon, and Japan did not immediately sue for peace. Why not?

The answer is involved, and exactly how this war ended is still the subject of controversy. This report represents a review of the record as found particularly in the memoirs of Truman, Stimson, McCloy, Byrnes, Leahy, Compton, the history of the Army Air Forces, and the story of Admiral (then Captain) Ellis M. Zacharias, who was in charge of psychological-warfare broadcasts to the Japanese.

It is not easy now to re-create the wartime emotional mood of those in command of the Japanese and American governments. This war had been ruthless, from the beginning shock of Pearl Harbor and the horror of the Bataan Death March. It had been a long and painful road through the bloody swamps of Guadalcanal and the other bitter islands, culminating in the smoking cities of the Empire. The ruthlessness and the length of the war made it difficult for either side to visualize sitting down to build a peace with the other side and, further, there were two irreconcilable attitudes maintained by the two opposing forces.

On one side was an alliance that had mobilized for a goal of unconditional surrender. On the other side was a power that in peace or war held a religious veneration for the head of its government. The Japanese could not imagine a world in which their institution of Emperor would be abolished. Nor could they have visualized Admiral Halsey, in the terms of his boast, "riding the Emperor's white horse down the streets of Tokyo." In this year of 1945 the Japanese had seen Germany and Italy bombed and defeated. They had seen Mussolini lynched, and Hitler a suicide, his body burned and lost in the ruins. The Japanese people simply could not think how their war might end.

The American people fully expected the Japanese Emperor to be overthrown and at least imprisoned, if not in fact executed as a war criminal. Of course, many prominent Americans were counseling against any such program. Joseph Grew, as we have seen, did his best to persuade the President, and Stimson notes that Grew and others were then being "roundly denounced as appeasers." Stimson, McCloy, and others agreed with Grew, however. And the subject was publicly discussed: for example, the Washington *Post* during this period was editorializing on unconditional surrender and the wisest ways of bringing the war to an end. But the Japanese government had a clear impression that the absolute and utter leveling of their government was the unalterable goal of the American people. Many times the Japanese rulers had made clear that they could never accept this, even unto the death of millions of their people in their own countryside.

This was the basic, apparently irreconcilable, situation as our land, sea, and air forces met daily in bloody combat.

To this situation the bomb added certain X factors of technical power. But our leaders did not feel certain of the effect this new weapon would have in terms of psychological power—i.e., political power.

Could this "X" force the Japanese to "bow to the inevitable"?

Had the Japanese already tried to surrender?

As we have seen, the Japanese Emperor had spoken to his cabinet on June 20, suggesting that they make ready an emergency plan for surrender. But that did not mean that most of the top rulers of the country were prepared to seriously consider such an alternative. There was, in fact, a split between the militaristic group that ran Japan and the Emperor and those close to him.

And it was only natural that the Japanese should be divided among themselves, or even within themselves. Even before June 20 there had been peace feelers out of Japan. But there had been no really clear-cut move.

In late May a prominent Japanese newspaperman, who had left Berlin before the final disaster, had sent messages to Foreign Minister Togo urging him to make peace overtures to avoid Germany's fate of having her cities blasted to bits. This newspaperman, Jiro Taguchi, even approached the United States Ambassador in Switzerland, Leland Harrison, and offered to find neutral intermediaries to work out a peace. Japanese businessmen in Berns supported Taguchi in his proposals. But these were still unofficial overtures. No matter what Japanese private citizens might wish, and no matter what they truly said about the uselessness of further destruction, their government continued to fight—and to inflict great damage upon us.

We were winning, but we were not coasting. Japan was losing the war, but she was not passive. She was wounding us, and this remained a costly and deadly war.

In April and May, Japan sent peace messages or peace propaganda over her radio, and she also sent messages through the Vatican (which acted merely as a transmittal agency). Our diplomatic and intelligence people went over every statement line by line, seeking to understand the true intentions of the Japanese. One verdict was that Japan's "line" was much too ambiguous. As one observer put it, the messages blew "hot and cold . . . today protesting Japan's determination and strength and tomorrow admitting complete exhaustion and failure." A "peace" message read today, when Japan and the United States are at peace, seems quite clear. But when, as was then the case, the overture for peace was sandwiched in between messages of defiance and accompanied by military action that hurt us, it did not seem so clear.

At the end of June a new Japanese Premier, Admiral Suzuki, made a speech to the Japanese parliament, the Diet, in which there were many undertones indicating a recognition that they were in a desperate situation and might think of surrender. It was also clear that he meant to be overheard by the world.

But what was his meaning?

> As bold as it may seem [the Premier said], I firmly believe there is no one in the entire world who is more deeply concerned with world peace and the welfare of mankind than His Imperial Majesty the Emperor. The brutal and inhuman acts of both America and England are aimed to make it impossible for us to follow our national policy as proclaimed by the Emperor Meiji. I hear that the enemy is boasting of his demand of unconditional surrender. . . . Unconditional surrender will only mean that our national structure and our people will be destroyed. Against such boastful talk there is only one measure we must take—that is to fight to the last.

The intelligence experts read these messages as carefully as they could. And if they found them ambiguous, they might conclude that they were meant to be ambiguous—with the hope of confusing our own purposes. In our own case, we sent many messages toward Japan with the express purpose of doing just that. It was hard to arrive at truth and clarity after years of deliberate and planned confusion.

But in June the Japanese Ambassador to the Kremlin had made representations to the Kremlin, as was reported by Stalin to his fellow conferees at Potsdam. That was official.

Did the Japanese not assume that Stalin would someday enter the war? Would he be friendly to a peace move? Did he fairly put their message to the West? Why would Stalin *want* to see that war end, before he had a chance to stake a claim in that part of Asia? Would he simply be relieved to find he did not have another war to fight? As early as April 8 Stalin had renounced his neutrality pact with Japan. In any case, as Stalin put it, the Japanese were not specific. As a matter of fact, they said *they wanted the West to be more specific,* to spell out just what we meant by "unconditional surrender." To Moscow on July 21 the Japanese Foreign Minister sent a message: "We cannot accept unconditional surrender under any circumstances."

Just what had we said about surrender, and what were we saying about it now?

Following the Potsdam Declaration, an intensive propaganda campaign had been waged by us against the Japanese. Millions of leaflets had been dropped, offering the terms we considered "honorable."

We had also named cities we intended to bomb—but we did not name Hiroshima. That was considered a prime military target and our military did not want the soldiers to flee. Our intelligence had reported on August 5 that 40,000 troops had just moved into the military headquarters there. Even now, many years later, there is no agreed figure on how many military personnel were killed, and there is still great disagreement as to how many thousands of civilians were killed. There was some agreement that at least 100,000 persons were dead, missing, or fatally injured after the Hiroshima bombing. But the last official United States figure says that only 3243 soldiers were killed, while a Japanese source says it was more like 40,000.

In any case, no one who knew the facts could doubt that here one bomb had destroyed one city.

Once again we dropped millions of leaflets. This time we said:

TO THE JAPANESE PEOPLE

We are in possession of the most destructive explosive ever devised by man. A single one of our newly developed atomic bombs is actually the equivalent in explosive power to what 2,000 of our giant B-29s can carry on a single mission. This awful fact is one for you to ponder and we solemnly assure you it is grimly accurate.

We have just begun to use this weapon against your homeland. If you still have any doubt, make inquiry as to what happened to Hiroshima when just one atomic bomb fell on that city.

Before using this bomb to destroy every resource of the military by which they are prolonging this useless war, we ask that you now petition the Emperor to end the war. Our President has outlined for you the thirteen consequences of an honorable surrender. We urge that you accept these consequences and begin the work of building a new, better, and peace-loving Japan.

You should take steps now to cease military resistance. Otherwise, we shall resolutely employ this bomb and all our other superior weapons to promptly and forcefully end the war.

While these leaflets were raining down on the Japanese, we also delivered some regular bombing attacks. The day after Hiroshima, a 131-plane mission struck Tokokawa. And the 509th, to keep on the alert, was also ordered to fly more practice missions and to drop more Pumpkins. The 509th had plenty of Pumpkins, but it did not have plenty of the new bombs. We did not, in fact, have at hand the means to follow up what we threatened, i.e., that we could "resolutely employ this bomb . . ."

However, the Japanese had no way of knowing that we had made only three atomic bombs and had exploded two of them, one in a test and one in action. Indeed, we later secured evidence that their high command did in fact assume that we had a supply and could do as we said.

But the Japanese still hesitated to surrender, unconditionally.

Admiral Zacharias has stated many times his belief, as he put it in his book *Secret Missions:*

> If the detailed interpretations of the unconditional surrender formula had been forthcoming in June rather than the end of July, the war would have ended without Soviet participation and before the dropping of the atomic bombs on Hiroshima and Nagasaki.

Zacharias, in his broadcasts and through other means he took to reach Japanese leaders, said:

> The Japanese leaders face two alternatives . . . one is the virtual destruction of Japan followed by a dictated peace. The other is unconditional surrender with its attendant benefits as laid down by the Atlantic Charter.

But the difference between "dictated peace" and "unconditional surrender" did not, then or now, seem as wide as the Pacific.

Zacharias told the Japanese:

> I know that unconditional surrender is a technical term which refers to *the form in which hostilities are terminated.* On the other hand, you know that the exact conditions of the *peace* are something to be settled in the future. Japan must make the next move.

Zacharias in another broadcast said that the Japanese themselves, and not the Americans, had introduced the idea of unconditional surrender into the war. He said that General Yamashita at Singapore and General Homma in the Philippines, had used such surrender as an instrument for "imposing submission and humiliation." But, he emphasized, "no such motive prompts the American peace formula."

But that summer, and in this first week of August, the Japanese did not seem to believe our broadcasts. Nor did they seem to understand other conciliatory words. They seemed only to hear the two fatal and unconciliatory words, and they felt the force of the continued bombings.

A member of the Japanese Foreign Office, Toshikazu Kase, in recounting the surrender story, has described the maneuvering going on behind the scenes in the Emperor's government. Kase attended key cabinet meetings seeking the final decisions of the war.

According to him, the Emperor and some advisers were already in a mood to negotiate and face surrender, but a militaristic faction was in control of the conduct of war and home-front information. Kase is supported by General Douglas MacArthur in the view that there was actual danger of an open split or a revolution in which the civilian government would have lost control and the Army would have fought on fanatically.

According to the United States Strategic Bombing Survey, which studied the surrender story immediately after the war's end, the Emperor, *before Hiroshima,* was disposed to accept the terms of the Potsdam Declaration. According to Kase, the militarists even deleted some of the "honorable terms" of the Potsdam Declaration, before they released the Declaration to the Japanese people. Thus the Emperor was not at all the dictator Mussolini and Hitler had been, but was to some extent the prisoner and captive of the war party in Tokyo. At the same time his protection was a supreme goal of his people. Hirohito at this moment appeared more of a symbol than the source of power.

So in this anomalous situation, the bomb was a symbol of an end to war, but it was not yet ending *this* war.

The Japanese Supreme War Council had to decide, on behalf of Japan, whether, or how, to end the war. This group consisted of three civilians and three military men. The latter were the War Minister and the two Chiefs of Staff.

The Foreign Minister advocated surrender, subject to one condition: keeping the Emperor.

The War Minister and the two Chiefs wanted to add other conditions: no occupation, no punishment of war criminals except by the Japanese government, and others.

Meanwhile the entire world was discussing the atomic bomb. Around the globe, politicians and priests—and generals—were saying that this final weapon meant an end to this war and all wars. But Japanese leaders, not without reason, felt they still could not agree on a program which could be accepted both by the Allies and also by the Japanese people.

At midnight on August 9 the Council held what was its most fateful meeting. The Emperor attended the meeting, but he did not preside and his attendance was considered more or less ceremonial. The Chairman was Admiral

Suzuki, a man who had the difficult task of trying to mediate between the military and political wings of the battered government of Japan. This night they were evenly divided.

While they met, another word, like "uranium," was being added to the world vocabulary of the new age.

On land, on sea, and in the air the war went on. The 509th had further refined its operating procedure on August 8, when it made a practice strike over the Empire and once again dropped pumpkin bombs.

The 509th was not scheduled to make another atomic-bomb strike until after August 11. But on Tinian the weather experts felt that they saw a bad Pacific storm on the way. The consensus was that the 509th had better fly now or they might not be able to fly for an indefinite period.

So on the 8th it was pumpkins, but the next day a new and more deadly thing was in a plane from the 509th, over the city of Kokura. This was the number-two city, and about 0930 on August 9, the plane made three passes over Kokura. Each time the pilot could not even see the city under the clouds, and the bombardier could not make the visual sighting demanded of these missions.

The plane—it was named after Captain Frederick C. Bock, and was called "Bock's Car"—gave up on the number-two city and headed for number three. That city, too, was overcast, but the bombardier found a hole in the clouds. He flipped the switch.

At 1058, August 9, the equations again proved correct. Mass was converted into energy into blast. Plutonium—that was the new word—plutonium was converted into radiation, into heat, and into light, blinding light.

That was Nagasaki.

No one had turned off the machine.

Some who think the human race can survive Hiroshima feel that Nagasaki was the fatal mistake that our race will not survive. Mistake it may have been, but apparently it was not an accident. Nagasaki was part of the design, according to official accounts.

The original plan had called for a list of five cities. The report in December, before Yalta, had said there would be a bomb, then another bomb sometime later, then others more frequently thereafter. However, it was to be many months before it could be announced that bombs were being made "on a production basis." Most records are still secret, and in the reports so far made public there is no hint that the 509th ever expected to have another bomb after Nagasaki. There is no record that Truman was personally informed of the bomb-production rate, or told that we had only two bombs. It does not seem likely that precise reports would have been given to him at the time.

Truman, some years later, recalled that from the *Augusta* he had given an order for *"two atomic bombs"* to be dropped.

Further, the idea that Japan should be threatened with a series of bombs was part of our policy at this time.

The announcement of the bomb, prepared before it was even known that Hiroshima would be the fatal city, had been designed to broadcast that threat as soon as the bomb was dropped. In that announcement Truman had said to Japan and the world:

> It was to spare the Japanese people from utter destruction that the ultimatum of July 26 was issued at Potsdam. Their leaders promptly rejected that ultimatum. If they do not now accept our terms, they may expect a rain of ruin from the air, the like of which has never been seen on this earth.

As Japan's Supreme War Council met with the Emperor, on August 9, they had just received the word of Nagasaki.

They were also reeling from the news that the Soviet had entered the war the night before. The Russians were moving into Manchuria; their guns and propaganda machinery were proceeding in a massive mobilization.

The Japanese War Minister still held his bloc together. They did not want to surrender. The meeting was deadlocked. Premier Suzuki would not break the tie by voting himself. It remained three-to-three. The split remained hopeless until 2:00 A.M. the following day.

Kase, an eyewitness, tells what happened then. Admiral Suzuki rose to his feet and quietly said:

> Gentlemen, we have spent hours in deliberation without coming to a decision and yet agreement is not in sight. You are fully aware that we cannot afford to waste even a minute at this juncture. I propose, therefore, to seek the imperial guidance and substitute it for the decision of this conference.

This was the first time the Emperor had been called on for an active part in such councils. He responded with decision.

He said there was but one choice before him: "to call a halt to the war and accept the Allies' terms, bearing what was indeed very hard to bear."

A message accepting the Potsdam Declaration was prepared. But there was still one condition attached: that the Emperor be kept, i.e., that the surrender treaty did not contain "any demand which prejudices the prerogatives of His Majesty as a sovereign ruler."

When acceptance of the Potsdam terms was announced on the Japanese radio, the Japanese military were angered, and Japan was quite close to revolution.

And in Washington the American high command also hesitated.

At 7:30 A.M. American radio monitors heard the news, as given to the Japanese. President Truman called a 9:00 A.M. meeting in his office to consider whether we could accept this conditional acceptance. Attending were Leahy, Byrnes, Stimson, and Forrestal.

Since Stimson had always felt we should let the Japanese keep their Emperor, he repeated it that morning. Leahy agreed, if for no reason other than the Emperor's usefulness in effecting an orderly surrender. Forrestal proposed a delicately worded reply, which would accept but still insist that the purposes of the Potsdam Declaration were to be accomplished.

Byrnes leaned toward the idea of unconditional, unequivocal surrender.

The President asked Byrnes to draft a reply along the lines proposed by Forrestal. This was done and submitted, with all possible speed that same day, to the President and then to our allies, Britain, China, and Russia.

Our reply said that "the authority of the Emperor and the Japanese Government . . . shall be subject to the Supreme Commander . . ."

There was another provision—that the Emperor would

be required to sign the surrender terms—but the British thought this unwise, and it was changed to read, "The Emperor will be required to authorize and ensure the signature . . ."

That message was sent through Switzerland the next day, August 11.

Meanwhile the war went on, and Admiral Chester Nimitz sent an order to all of the Pacific fleet that the proposals and counter-proposals "must not be permitted to affect vigilance . . . neither the Japanese nor Allied Forces have stopped fighting . . . Offensive action shall be continued. . . ."

August 12 was a Sunday, but all day the President and Secretary Byrnes, often joined by members of the high military command, waited nervously for a Japanese answer. It did not come that day or the next.

In Japan the Emperor wanted to accept the American reply, but the Japanese military was ablaze. A military group was planning a coup d'état, thinking of capturing the Emperor and cabinet and planning to continue all-out war.

The rebels bombed the residence of the Foreign Minister, who had led the surrender wing. But the cabinet formally ratified the Emperor's decision on the afternoon of August 14. Then a group of Army rebels actually gained control of the Palace. They were looking for a phonograph recording—the first the Emperor had ever made—which was to be played on the Japanese radio, announcing Japan's defeat. They did not find the record.

Amid such confusion the final Japanese message was sent through Switzerland to Washington and delivered to Secretary Byrnes by the Swiss Chargé d'Affaires:

"His Majesty the Emperor has issued an imperial rescript

regarding Japanese acceptance of the provisions of the Potsdam Declaration . . ."

This message, like ours, to which it replied, implied that the Emperor would be the head of government for an unspecified time. The two statements, masterpieces of calculated ambiguity, did not say the Emperor would stay and did not say he would go. The Japanese reply did not state any conditions, but still it did not say they surrendered unconditionally. Yet that was implied by acceptance of the Potsdam Declaration.

That night the President gathered the White House correspondents and announced that the war was over. The news went immediately to the crowds gathered in downtown Washington and in all the major cities of America. The V-J celebration went on through the night.

Said the President, "I deem this reply a full acceptance of the Potsdam Declaration which specified the unconditional surrender of Japan. In the reply there is no qualification."

It was done.

The two cities of Hiroshima and Nagasaki lay flat and black and still. There was very little movement, except where some remains of the great fires still smoldered.

Some Japanese survivors who had apparently been uninjured still walked around. They did not realize that they would be dead shortly, that within them there still smoldered the effects of invisible radiation. Unknowingly, these walking dead thought the bomb was finished. They did not know that in one way—physically—it would *never* be finished, that many who survived would transmit defects to generation upon generation.

This genetic effect was an unknown factor in the bombs, a symbol of the other unknown factors—the social and political effects that these actions were to have upon the life of man.

At the moment, all around the world, millions of men and women were celebrating the end of the war. For the first time in years most of the world's soldiers could plan for the quiet of peace.

Millions were shocked at the surprise we gave the Japanese, but few men knew of the other surprises which radiation and the bomb would have for all of us. Whether they were asleep or shocked awake, all men through these events had moved from the shadow of the war to the shadow of the bomb. In this way we began the atomic world in which our children and their children must find their way.

"Give order that these bodies
High on a stage be placed to the view;
And let me speak to the yet unknowing world
How these things came about: so shall you hear
Of carnal, bloody, and unnatural acts,
Of accidental judgments, casual slaughters,
Of deaths put on by cunning and forced cause,
And, in this upshot, purposes mistook
Fallen on the inventors' heads. . . .
But let this same be presently performed,
Even while men's minds are wild; lest more mischance
On plots and errors happen."

—Horatio, in the last scene of
Hamlet, Prince of Denmark.

19.

Conscience and Questions

THE DREAMS OF victory ended with the reality of achievement, and ever since we have been troubled by the face that victory wore. Nightmares of war ended and we found that there would be nightmares of peace. Men began to think that a world of security would never be achieved in the new age.

We look back, with troubling questions, at these events, which helped so much to set new limits and choices for man. Were the atomic bombings necessary for an early end to the Pacific war? Were the atomic bombs used in haste, without proper thought of the consequences?

This book was written to help people answer these questions for themselves. There is also a hope that if the available record is set down, as far as it can be, other people who have not yet spoken may tell the full story of their participation. There are official records that should be opened now. Some contain no official secrets. Others contain technical secrets now outmoded. It is time for these records to be opened, but, so far, the doors have remained shut to journalists, historians, and sometimes to former officials, even to famous American officials who lived through these events. A nation, like a man, cannot fully understand its future if it does not understand some of the secrets of the past.

Still today I have felt there was enough in the record now to make this story worth while. And it is possible and proper to review some of the questions that may be on the conscience of Americans and others. In considering the material in this chapter the writer would ask the reader to remember that in the rest of the book he has tried to keep his own opinions out of the story, but in this chapter we deal, to some extent, with the author's conclusions and conjectures.

Who made the decision to drop the bomb as it was dropped?

Mr. Truman made the decision, and mainly he followed the recommendations of Mr. Stimson and the Interim Committee. However, at Potsdam some major changes were made in the A-bomb policy; for example, in the matter of "a clear warning." To this writer, it is not apparent that the Potsdam Declaration gave the Japanese any clue of the coming revolution in weapons. What happened, at Potsdam, to this idea of a warning?

Was this an American decision, or was it a decision of the Allies, with Britain as a partner?

As we have seen, the British sent official word of their consent to use of the bomb, on July 4, and at the Potsdam meeting Churchill again gave consent for his government. Their agreement is in the public record. There is thus an official effort to make this seem to be a joint decision.

Yet Truman always refers to the decision as if it were one made solely by this government, and personally made by him.

To this writer, it seems it was not really a joint decision. Nor was it a separate action taken without regard to the Alliance. It was an American decision, but it was agreed to by Churchill, and it was made by Truman.

In the opinion of many observers, the world would be a far safer place if we could have counted then, and now, on thorough consultation between nations before such new developments are launched. Usually, as in the case of the "blind bombers" proposed for bombing Germany, during Truman's first week in office, consultation promotes caution.

Should we have dropped the bomb as we did?

Knowing the facts now available, the writer's judgment is that we should never have dropped the bomb without clear warning, or without a demonstration of it on an uninhabited territory, or without giving time for us and the enemy to understand something of what it meant. The action as it was taken was not in the long-range interests of this country, or of humanity.

In this history, all these qualifications were urged by many of the scientists, and two of them were urged by Stimson. In the press of events these factors were simply neither properly heard nor fully understood, in the writer's opinion.

The writer's personal convictions, however, are that we Americans were quite unrealistic in our statements about unconditional surrender and that we were quite ruthless in adopting a policy of area bombing. The writer agrees with the attitude which Captain Harry Butcher attributes to General Eisenhower in World War II, that all surrenders are conditional. And the writer agrees with Admiral Leahy that mass bombing of women and children takes us back to the days of Genghis Khan. We said it was barbarous when Hitler did it, and we were right.

But still another question should be asked: *How much was the thinking of Truman and Stimson limited and conditioned by the desperate pressures of those days?*

In a word, does this decision reflect these men's best judgment—or their best judgment under pressure?

Perhaps a complete answer on this main question would be—no, you or I would probably not have so swiftly and arbitrarily changed the world, *if we had understood the potential.* With thirteen years' more knowledge you would not have ordered the first bomb dropped, as it was. But if you had stood where Stimson and Truman stood, with the knowledge they had at the time, your decision might have been much the same as theirs. Giving the decision more thought than many others did at the time, they acted in good faith.

This good faith does not validate everything which the principals have said by way of justification since then. Good or bad conscience, of course, does not establish that in fact this weapon *was* the decisive factor in ending the war and saving lives. But the author has no doubt that Truman and the men advising him thought it could be the decisive factor. In that light they did their duty as they saw it.

The writer finds that all the principals, years after, still seem to be uneasy about this decision.

To this writer, this uneasy feeling comes from these people in many ways, in later years. In 1958 when Mr. Truman speaks of the bomb decision, he seems fantastically certain, just as Oppenheimer seems uncertain and hesitant, about Hiroshima or later bomb decisions. Stimson detailed quite clearly the questions he kept asking himself years later. Why could he not forget them?

One psychological point is this: at the time, in this author's opinion, their consciences were more clear than they are now. For good or ill, this was not a thing of premeditation. And there were later doubts as to the practical ends as well as moral consequences of these acts.

Did the bombs win the war or did they merely "close" the war?

Many military men answer that Japan was already defeated. They say both Hiroshima and Nagasaki were militarily unnecessary.

Various services of the government still claim that their particular efforts won the war, regardless of the bomb. One has to remember, however, the partisan bias of each service. To some extent, Navy strategists conclude that the naval blockade could have won the war. Airmen feel even more strongly that their aerial bombardment of Japan made the surrender inevitable. People who were managing the psychological broadcasts against the Japanese in the spring and summer of 1945 believe that their interpretation to the Japanese of a more reasonable meaning to unconditional surrender was quite influential. In fact, many believe the psychological approach was a necessary ingredient of the final surrender.

The Russians, of course, in their press made a great thing of the fact that they entered the war in the Pacific and, presto, that war was over! At first glance, this seems ridiculous. However, even some Americans have believed that it was in fact quite important to the Japanese to know that from that point on they would be fighting a two-front war.

Some surrender importance was attached by some of our own people to the threat of a Russian campaign.

Japan's surrender was quite different from that of Germany. Although Japan had been badly bombed and her casualties had been enormous, she did not go all the way to the bitter end. Nazi Germany did not really surrender, it collapsed utterly. Japan stopped short of total disintegration, and consequently one can find support for a theory that she "should" have surrendered much earlier, or one can find support for the theory that she could have gone on for some indefinite time.

Personally, without exhaustive study of the complicated surrender story, the writer believes Japan was beaten, but was not ready to surrender until the bomb. The bomb gave an excuse or reason to Japan for surrender close to our terms.

And this writer has a theory which no one else has expressed: It gave Americans another reason, too. We Americans, on hearing of the bomb, were more willing to see the war end, even if we made some concessions to the Japanese, as in the matter of their Emperor.

Was Hiroshima a military target?

In the words of Truman, according to the book, *Mr. President,* "I had told Stimson that the bomb should be dropped as nearly as possible upon a war production center of military importance."

Nagasaki, home of an important Mitsubishi Works, was far more of an industrial center, and some have thought Hiroshima was a departure from "military bombing."

Hiroshima was a port of embarkation, frequently filled with troops, and also had war industry. The turn in policy which developed "area bombing" had been made some months earlier. That went far beyond what would have been called "military targets" at the start of the war, and parts of Hiroshima would have been targets under a more narrow definition.

It appears that the American public then or later did not realize that we had already adopted a policy of bombing entire districts with high explosives and incendiaries. Hiroshima was the first such raid in which this policy was clearly seen by the whole world.

The number of civilians killed at Hiroshima shocked the air power command, as it shocked Oppenheimer and others. This was not planned. It appears that we did not, in fact, have any idea that the city would be so unprotected. We sent only three planes, because any more might perhaps have brought out dangerous antiaircraft or fighter planes in counter-attack. As a result of avoiding this attack, we inadvertently achieved another effect in that the Japanese did not set off the air-raid alarm that would have driven the Hiroshima citizens to shelter.

That accidental happening cost the lives of tens of thousands of women and children who were not military targets and whom we had no intention of killing.

When was the Franck Report actually delivered to the office of the Secretary of War?

Did Stimson give real consideration to the arguments of Franck and his friends? If the Report arrived before the meeting of the Interim Committee, he had time. But if it did not arrive until much later, as members of the Franck Committee have told me, he was then on his way to Potsdam.

The answer to this factual question would tell us a good

deal about the kind of consideration given to certain alternatives to dropping the bomb as it was dropped. Dr. Compton has a firm recollection that it was delivered before the May 31 meeting of the Interim Committee. Members of the Franck Committee have written or informed me that the report was not even finished by that time. Compton has recently been over his own notes and many of the official records of those days, and is giving his best recollection. Files will have to be opened before this point can be cleared up to the satisfaction of everyone.

Meanwhile Dr. Franck, in 1958, asked the present writer to emphasize that he felt the atomic decision had been made by "responsible men," and that the differences between the policy his committee recommended and the policy the government adopted did not mean that he, Franck, felt that their decision was hasty or taken without due consideration.

Oppenheimer has written in 1958 that he has often wondered if the decisions taken "that June" had been different, would the history of the postwar world have been far different? His own conclusion is that history would have taken much the same course, that the cold war and the postwar world would have developed in much the same way.

In this passage Oppenheimer does not make clear what decisions and what subsequent history he had in mind. One may assume that he refers to the decision to drop the bomb on a populated target without warning, and of the development of many kinds of bombs and many kinds of wars since 1945.

The atomic age has changed all man's future—but how much was changed by these two bombs dropped in this particular way?

The Franck Report asked men to think about history, before using the bomb. Who really read it? When?

Did Stalin understand what Truman meant to tell him about the bomb?

This is at present a mystery, but not one which could not be cleared up. Russian historians might do so, if they felt like it, or Americans might clarify it with further statements from those who were at Potsdam.

According to the available memoirs, the President definitely meant to tell Stalin we had an extraordinary weapon. But Truman did not use the word "atom."

The secret agents of the Russian government, men like Gold, Fuchs, Greenglass, Pontecorvo, and Nunn May, had been busy on our atomic project for a long time. Did Stalin gather enough from Truman's words to understand that a new force was coming into the world? Had Stalin learned enough from his technical advisers to perceive what the President was talking about? Can we be certain that Russian scientific intelligence reached the top of the Kremlin?

The answers would tell us something about the importance our supposed atomic monopoly had upon the Russian attitude toward us as the cold war began.

The USSR had kept many secrets from its Allies, but so far as we know, it possessed nothing then of the significance of the atomic weapons secret. Were the men in the Kremlin startled and shocked by our manufacture and use of the new weapon without full clearance with them? They never protested to the West. Does their silence indicate no shock, or does it indicate extreme shock?

We look back at Stalin's enigmatic smile at Potsdam, and wonder about three possibilities. He hoodwinked the West.

Or we hoodwinked him. Or else, we gave and he took the intelligence as normal business. We told him we had a tremendous weapon, he knew what it was, he urged us to use it, and we did.

It must be remembered that there was no means by which we could have used this weapon in the European war in which Russia was then our ally. We were telling Stalin about a weapon we were going to use in our war. In the Pacific, the Russians were not yet in action, although they were committed to join us.

Did Russia hurry into the war because she knew of the bomb? The writer does not believe she did. Did she hold back, because she knew the bombs would cut her participation short? It seems unlikely.

Did we hurry? That is our next question.

Were the first atomic bombs really "aimed" at Russia, not Japan?

There are those who say we finished and dropped this bomb as speedily as we could, with Russia and the beginning cold war as the incentive for haste. They say that we had the goals of keeping Russia out of any share in the Pacific victory, and of threatening Russia with our power in the postwar world. In this interpretation, Truman's remark, as reported by Jonathan Daniels, "I'll have a hammer on those boys," might be considered quite important.

P. M. S. Blackett, a Nobel-Prize-winning British physicist, has summarized this belief: "The dropping of the atomic bombs was not so much the last military act of the second world war, as the first major operation of the cold diplomatic war with Russia."

This implies that our national leaders at this time were

already quite well informed as to the political and diplomatic potential of atomic energy. It implies further that they had thought through some of the main implications of postwar foreign relations, and put these thoughts together with the probable course of atomic development; beyond that, they had then agreed upon a policy. This writer believes that, on the contrary, the high commanders had hardly had time to consider or plan for the atomic potential. We may have dropped this bomb in such a way that the timing injured the Russian position in the Far East. But it is not clear that this factor was involved in the decision.

This history shows that the atomic weapon had hardly been synchronized with military operations, much less integrated with future political and diplomatic aims. This conclusion does not imply that this would have been an unworthy national goal on our part, i.e., to end the war before Russia could have been brought in. Such a move would have saved bloodshed, presumably, and it would be hard in retrospect to argue that we should have waited indefinitely for Russia to come in, as an ally. We had already waited for years. She had military reasons for staying out. We had military reasons for dropping the bomb. It can much more reasonably be argued that the timing of the bombs, particularly the second so close after the first, injured our position in the Far East. The author's personal observation is that many Asians and Americans afterward thought differently about Western man's supposed respect for human life. These bombs did not improve our reputation and win us allies in Asia.

At any time between Pearl Harbor and Hiroshima, British and American military leaders were eager to have Russia in action in the Pacific. Their arguments were similar to those with which the Russians urged upon us the opening of a Second Front in Europe. It is true that in 1945, in the closing months of the war, a few men (like Byrnes) would have been happier if Russia were not planning to enter the Pacific war. But what did Byrnes or the others do about it? At Potsdam they continued to plan for Russian entry.

Many years later General Groves looked back to claim what he regarded as a foresighted position on Russia. He told the board in the Oppenheimer hearings:

> I think it important to state that there was never from about two weeks from the time I took charge of the project any illusion on my part but that Russia was the enemy and that the project was conducted on that basis. I didn't go along with the attitude of the country as a whole that Russia was a gallant ally. I always had suspicions and the project was conducted on that basis. Of course, that was reported to the President.

There are several things to be said against this as evidence of an anti-Russian atomic policy. For one thing, as can be said of several other statements quoted in our story, it represents a man looking back, after some years, to say what his beliefs were at a given time. And this statement of Groves does not check very well, in this writer's judgment, with the conclusions expressed on the record at the time by those more responsible for making the decision. Stimson never speaks of wartime views on Russia as an enemy.

As for Russia's timetable, there is some evidence that she hurried up her entrance, after Hiroshima. But she arrived in action almost to the day and hour which she had promised many months earlier. Long before this she had been committed to come in three months after Hitler was defeated. Her planned entrance was a secret, but much more widely known to the allied command than the secret atomic bomb. It does not appear that any of the military authorities in the hot Japanese war were much preoccupied with the coming cold war.

There is no evidence to show that the high command anticipated that this weapon could end the war abruptly. Military opinion is still divided as to just how Japan was defeated, as we have seen. We do not know whether Stalin really understood, at this time, what atomic weapons might mean. If all the information from his own scientists, Fuchs, and other agents, had made a deep impression on him, did that have a bearing on his entering the war? We don't know.

The writer does not know of any convincing evidence that the bomb drop was a move against Russia.

How significant was the information given by the spies to Russia? Was it crucial to Russia's own atomic effort?

The universal judgment of scientists and engineers seems to be that it was within Russian capabilities and natural resources to go ahead and make the A-bomb and later the H-bomb without any information whatever from espionage in the West.

In other words, we should not conclude that if there had been no spies Russia would not have had the bomb. Nor should we feel that without Gold and Fuchs, she could not have made the bomb for ten or twenty years, that it would have taken her much longer to match our effort. The spies saved time for the Russians, but not that much time.

The real question, then, is whether the information from

the spies advanced the Russian atomic timetable by an important period of time.

The Joint Committee on Atomic Energy of the U. S. Congress in a special report on this subject said that the combined activities of the spies "advanced the Soviet atomic program by eighteen months at a minimum." This would be an important period of time in power politics if it were felt that the world situation changed materially after the Americans ceased to have a monopoly on atomic weapons.

This estimate of eighteen months, moreover, is not unquestioned. Many feel that it is close to fantasy to place any such time estimate upon things of this sort. Others think it is very difficult to transmit important atomic information in a few pages or even in a few packets passing from one enemy agent to another. The general feeling among scientists is that the "secrets" of atomic energy production are not of a sort that can be written down or drawn out by a machinist such as Greenglass, nor even summed up in a few reports from brilliant men like Fuchs, or Bruno Pontecorvo. The "secrets" of atomic production, they say, would actually take an entire library. They could not be transported in a diplomatic pouch, but would require an entire merchant ship to carry them.

Yet the scientists generally agree that the knowledge that a particular process can be done at all is quite important to anyone setting out to duplicate it.

At the end of the war we told the whole world that we had made an atomic bomb. That information itself was quite important to anyone who had been thinking about the theoretical possibility. The same thing applies to subordinate manufacturing processes. Millions of dollars were spent upon the process to separate U-235 from U-238 through the phenomenon known as "gaseous diffusion." There were two other methods of separation and all three of these methods worked and were referred to in the official Smyth Report. This was quite important news to anyone setting out to make a bomb.

Surely it was important that Fuchs, who had worked on this very process of gaseous diffusion and who had known about Oak Ridge, had already reported these salient facts secretly to Gold long before they were "revealed" in the Smyth Report. Surely it was not unimportant that Fuchs could have had news of successful experiments about as quickly as anyone in the Los Alamos area. For example, he was in on the discussions of the basic theory which led to the hydrogen bomb.

Reports, drawings, and equations in small packages are not much to convey the complexities of modern science. It is often said the best way to send scientific information is to send it in the package of a human being, a first-class scientist. But in Pontecorvo (who disappeared into Russia after the war) and Fuchs, the Russians came in contact with two excellent packages, two walking encyclopedias of nuclear knowledge. The fact that these men were available and could be asked questions would probably not seem important, in the Sunday supplement concept of espionage in which spies deliver a few diagrams which, in the twinkling of an eye, permit the enemy to duplicate what has been done. But it surely was important that these men knew the general areas of doubt and of certainty in the new atomic world, that they knew not only the problems that had been solved, but the kinds of problems which came up.

They must also have known something about what kind of organization it takes to do this blend of military-scientific work.

So the answer as to the importance of the Fuchs-Greenglass-Gold-Rosenberg information might be that it was not all-important. It is simply not true that the Russian scientific effort rested mainly upon facts stolen from the West.

On the other hand, scientists who are understandably embittered by the disloyalty of certain scientists or the stupidities of our "loyalty system" have sometimes overstated the case for the utter unimportance of this espionage information. It was not unimportant to us when Leo Szilard and Eugene Wigner and Bruno Pontecorvo and Enrico Fermi and Klaus Fuchs came from Europe to work on the British-American project. And it was not unimportant when Pontecorvo and Fuchs, along with Gold and others, decided that they would tell all that they knew to the Russians.

Did we make the Potsdam Declaration clear enough and did we allow the Japanese enough time to think it over?

The facts are that on July 26 we gave the Japanese an ultimatum and we asked them to accept the terms of the Potsdam Declaration. They first refused, and then accepted, the terms of the Potsdam Declaration. They and we had avoided the explicit addition of a provision to keep the Emperor. Yet both sides apparently understood that the Emperor would stay on indefinitely.

Some people believe that the bomb worked as a specific instrument. We gave an ultimatum. It was not accepted. In fact the Japanese spoke in contempt of it, on July 28. Then we dropped the A-bombs and almost immediately they accepted the Potsdam terms. At the same time both sides had an understanding about the Emperor. To some it appears simple: the bomb changed them from NO to YES. But many people feel that it does not do real justice to the complexities of the situation. There is evidence that the Japanese merely meant to stall with their press statement of July 28. They thought they had more time, and their peace party needed time in which to work.

We offered the Japanese our terms, which they accepted in less than three weeks. What if we had given them three weeks to think over the terms, and had not dropped either bomb? We cannot know now, whether more time might not have done what seemed to have been done with more bombs.

Was the Nagasaki bomb necessary or important to ending the war?

This appears to the writer to be one of the most tragic ifs of our time.

Both Arthur Compton and his brother, the late Karl Compton, served with the Interim Committee which considered such questions. Years later, they still felt that it was not merely one bomb, but the threat of a series of bombs which gave Japan a good excuse for surrender.

However, this writer would argue that the three days beween the first two bombs was not enough time for the Japanese government to think over the implications of the new weapon and to take action to end the war before Nagasaki.

In the official records, such as Truman's descriptions, this writer imagines that he sees between the lines some regrets that the second bomb was dropped so soon after the first. There is no evidence that policy leaders held any high-policy meeting before the second bomb. The decision as to when it was to go was made "operationally." The order to the 509th spoke of "bombs." It said nothing about holding off if the news carried reports of surrender overtures from Japan. It said nothing about awaiting further orders for a second bomb. Truman's recollection is that on the *Augusta* returning from Potsdam he gave orders for two bombs. This writer takes Truman's intention at 100 per cent but does not believe the Truman memory has proved 100 per cent correct. History's final judgments must rest on original documents, not upon memory. Such an order, if it exists, has not been available to this writer. Until the records are opened, until we can see some explicit order on the second bomb, this writer assumes the military commanders in the Pacific actually decided *when* to fire the second atomic bomb, as the plane commander decided *where*.

Would the Japanese have surrendered much earlier if the terms had explicitly included the keeping of the Emperor?

McCloy still asks this question and he, like others, is inclined to answer: Yes, they would have ended the war.

This is another speculative question, and many American officials would disagree. Surely many Japanese officials were opposed to ending the war at all costs. In Germany we had already made clear our war criminal policy: That courts of our own making would try and execute war criminals. Some Japanese leaders, therefore, knew their lives would likely be forfeit after a surrender.

It seems tragic that the Japanese never told us and we never asked them: Would you surrender on this condition?

Looking back, one can see that leaders on either side might have taken the initiative and saved themselves and the world a great deal of destruction and agony.

Grew, Stimson, McCloy, and many men in uniform who were familiar with Asia (such as Captain Zacharias) came to feel that a grave error of our surrender policy was in not negotiating about the Emperor and conditional surrender sooner than we did.

If we had made a moderate surrender proposal in June when the Emperor was talking to his cabinet about preparing a surrender program, the Japanese might have accepted. If so, both sides would have saved thousands of soldiers and civilians, and the A-bomb would not have been introduced to the world as a weapon already used in war.

What was Russia's reaction to the bombings?

This writer has gone over (in translation) what the Russian press had to say about the bomb for six months after Hiroshima. The overwhelming fact is that they said almost nothing of it, and gave their people the clear impression that Russia's entrance was the decisive factor in ending the war. Was this just a front they put up for their people? In the main, this writer believes it was, and that the leaders of the Kremlin knew the bomb had closed the war.

But there is much more to a proper understanding of the bomb than knowing just that.

My own belief is that the Russian national leaders, like ours, did not appreciate the importance of a national atomic policy this early in the atomic age. In the early years, the Russian world position was not improved by our apparent atomic monopoly, and Russia very likely could wish we had not used the bomb as we did. But I do not think her leaders would have expressed appreciation at the time, for the merits of a negotiated peace between the United States and Japan.

Few Americans did, but in the end and in great haste that is what we got. Today few Americans or Japanese would say, on reading the record, that we might not have achieved peace sooner with more thoughtfulness, and with more hope for the East and the West to truly understand each other.

Are governments today better equipped to act wisely when they have received news of revolutionary developments from science?

What men will make tomorrow's weapons decisions?

Will the world's third combat atomic bomb be exploded through the decision of a military commander in some local situation?

These are the questions of most importance for today. They must be answered.

Today's world is far more explosive than the world of 1945. Uranium bombs, plutonium bombs and hydrogen bombs are scattered in strategic locations around the globe. Every major city in the world is now on a list—your city is on some military commander's list. In some cases the live bombs are carried in patrolling planes. They are already in the air, on the alert, awaiting the command.

In the United States, so far as is known, only the military commanders of the defense have the authority to order atomic bombs to be dropped. These defense commanders already have the authority to use these bombs under certain conditions. Otherwise, we are to assume that any use of atomic bombs would be a decision for the highest authorities in the White House, the State Department and the Defense Department. But few men know how this decision would be made, if it were to be made again.

The atomic issue itself came up during the Korean war and figured in the differences between Mr. Truman and General Douglas MacArthur. It should be clear that since the war we have faced many kinds of provocation and have not used our ultimate weapon. The same may be said of the other atomic powers.

But even if all the great powers have refrained from using atomic or hydrogen bombs, this still does not answer the question of whether governments are today prepared to understand new knowledge about the world and the universe, as that knowledge comes from the laboratories. Would we, or they, use a brand-new weapon if it presented itself? Will human beings go on trying to achieve surprise—and then be themselves surprised? Will human arrogance continue to seek to shock other human beings, unthinking of the mysteries of the unknown in nature and the unknown of tomorrow?

Perhaps all these questions are aspects of the old question: Does man learn from history?

Some decisions of history are made with much more care than those of Hiroshima and Nagasaki, but perhaps some momentous decisions will always be made like this. One of these days such a decision may be fatal to our race. You may judge for yourself whether men will proceed in courage and ignorance, charity and rashness, so long as men make history.

The Great Decision

Since Hiroshima we may still use the phrase, *so long as men make history,* but by that we no longer mean forever.

Our forever and our future were changed at Hiroshima, they were involved in the great accident or the great decision.

Index

Index